# 30 YEARS THROUGH THE NEWS/LENS

## I Dedicate This Book to

*The many friends I've made during the 30 years I've been at the helm of The Rockport Pilot. From the everyday Joe to the true power figures, and even to those who wanted to be power figures, you all played a pivotal part in making publishing a community newspaper anything but boring.*

*The History Center for Aransas County, which I've chosen to benefit from all proceeds made through the sales of this book. History is recorded in newspapers, and I hope 30 Years Through the News/Lens is just one of many historic artifacts in the History Center 100 years from now.*

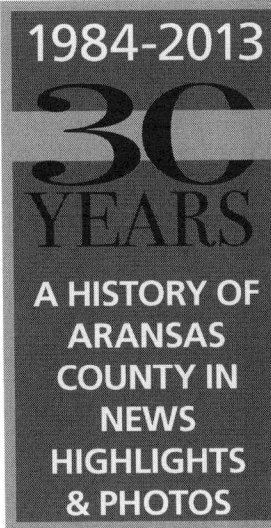

## THROUGH THE NEWS/LENS

# Mike Probst

Editor
and Publisher of
*The Rockport Pilot*

PRINTED IN THE UNITED STATES OF AMERICA

# 30 YEARS THROUGH THE NEWS/LENS

Copyright © 2014 Mike Probst
All rights reserved.
ISBN-13: 978-1502302106
ISBN-10: 1502302101
Library of Congress Control Number: 2014917099

Published by MJP3 Publishing, Rockport, Texas
Printed by CreateSpace Independent Publishing Platform,
North Charleston, SC

Design: Dawn Gwin Studio
Cover Photos: Mike Probst
Inside Photos: Mike Probst,
*The Rockport Pilot* staff, and contributing photographers

Available from Amazon.com and other retail outlets

First Printing: October 2014
Printed in the United States of America

*The Friends of the History Center of Aransas County
wish to thank the
Margaret Sue Rust Foundation
for their financial support for the
"Newseum" Exhibit mounted in collaboration
with the publication of
"30 Years Through the News/Lens".*

# CONTENTS

| | | | |
|---|---|---|---|
| Key | | | 7 |
| Forward | | | 8 |
| Introduction: My Story | | | 10 |
| Chapter 1 | Year 1 | 1984 | 17 |
| Chapter 2 | Year 2 | 1985 | 25 |
| Chapter 3 | Year 3 | 1986 | 33 |
| Chapter 4 | Year 4 | 1987 | 39 |
| Chapter 5 | Year 5 | 1988 | 47 |
| Chapter 6 | Year 6 | 1989 | 56 |
| Chapter 7 | Year 7 | 1990 | 65 |
| Chapter 8 | Year 8 | 1991 | 74 |
| Chapter 9 | Year 9 | 1992 | 82 |
| Chapter 10 | Year 10 | 1993 | 91 |
| Chapter 11 | Year 11 | 1994 | 99 |
| Chapter 12 | Year 12 | 1995 | 107 |
| Chapter 13 | Year 13 | 1996 | 118 |
| Chapter 14 | Year 14 | 1997 | 127 |
| Chapter 15 | Year 15 | 1998 | 138 |
| Chapter 16 | Year 16 | 1999 | 150 |
| Chapter 17 | Year 17 | 2000 | 161 |
| Chapter 18 | Year 18 | 2001 | 174 |
| Chapter 19 | Year 19 | 2002 | 186 |
| Chapter 20 | Year 20 | 2003 | 196 |
| Chapter 21 | Year 21 | 2004 | 207 |
| Chapter 22 | Year 22 | 2005 | 220 |
| Chapter 23 | Year 23 | 2006 | 230 |

# 30 YEARS THROUGH THE NEWS/LENS

| | | |
|---|---|---|
| Chapter 24 | Year 24 | 2007 ............................................. 241 |
| Chapter 25 | Year 25 | 2008 ............................................. 252 |
| Chapter 26 | Year 26 | 2009 ............................................. 262 |
| Chapter 27 | Year 27 | 2010 ............................................. 274 |
| Chapter 28 | Year 28 | 2011 ............................................. 287 |
| Chapter 29 | Year 29 | 2012 ............................................. 303 |
| Chapter 30 | Year 30 | 2013 ............................................. 316 |
| Acknowledgments | | ............................................. 327 |
| Special Thanks | | ............................................. 331 |

# KEY TO ABBREVIATIONS

AC ............... Aransas County
ACEMS ........ Aransas County Emergency Medical Services
ACMSI ......... Aransas County Medical Services Inc.
ACISD .......... Aransas County Independent School District
ACND .......... Aransas County Navigation District
ACSO ........... Aransas County Sheriff's Office
ANWR ......... Aransas National Wildlife Refuge
DPS .............. Department of Public Safety
FVFD ............ Fulton Volunteer Fire Department
HOT ............. Hotel Occupancy Tax
MP ............... Mike Probst, *Rockport Pilot* editor & publisher
P&Z ............. Planning and Zoning Commission
RCA ............. Rockport Center for the Arts
RCC ............. Rockport Country Club
RFCC ........... Rockport-Fulton Chamber of Commerce
RFHS ............ Rockport-Fulton High School
RFJHS ........... Rockport-Fulton Junior High School
RFMS ........... Rockport-Fulton Middle School
RP ................ *The Rockport Pilot*
RPD ............. Rockport Police Department
RVFD ........... Rockport Volunteer Fire Department
SH 35 .......... State Highway 35
TMM ........... Texas Maritime Museum
TPWD ......... Texas Parks and Wildlife Department
TxDOT ......... Texas Department of Transportation

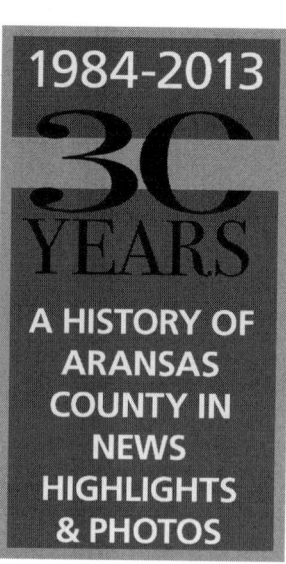

## THROUGH THE NEWS/LENS

## FORWARD

When I approached my 20th year at *The Rockport Pilot* my wife encouraged me to write a book about my experiences as a community newspaper publisher. The same thing happened as I approached my 25th year.

I figured I was off the hook as my 30th year at the helm drew near, but how wrong I was.

One Christmas gift from my family in 2013 was an "invitation" to write a book for the new History Center for Aransas County.

There was no way I could get out of it. My wife had just published her first book, and now it was my turn.

Little did I know how much work would be involved, but you now have in your possession the product of countless hours of writing, editing, scanning 30-year-old negatives, and of course, letting go and allowing others to help.

Once I got in the mood for putting together this book, a chronological history of Aransas County as

## FORWARD

published in the pages of *The Rockport Pilot*, it was all she wrote (pun intended).

I'm particularly proud of all the photographs my staff, contributing photographers, and I have taken through the years. This book includes more than 160 pictures, which were either published in the *Pilot*, or were in the same batch of photos taken at a particular event.

My biggest holdup was not gathering information, editing, etc., but rather sitting around going through pictures and reflecting on the years gone by.

Whenever the day comes to retire, who knows, I might start writing action thrillers, with a fictional twist, about things, which occurred in Aransas County!

In the meantime, I hope you enjoy reading these pages, and reliving old memories, as much as I enjoyed putting it together for you.

# 30 YEARS THROUGH THE NEWS/LENS

## *Introduction*

I didn't realize I had ink in my blood at an early age, but I guess I did.

I was born October 30, 1959 in New Orleans, well, actually, my birth certificate reads "rural Jefferson Parish," because the hospital where I was born wasn't in the city limits.

My dad, now a retired Lutheran minister, accepted a call in 1964 to a new church in El Paso.

It was in El Paso where I first dipped my fingers in printer's ink.

In the mid-60s, using a manual AB Dick mimeograph machine at my dad's church, I published and sold a neighborhood newspaper on 8-1/2 x 11 sheets of paper. The newspapers, which included "local news," recipes from mothers in the neighborhood, and seek-a-word puzzles and crossword puzzles, which I created, were sold door-to-door for a nickel.

I would try to sell anything to make a little money to spend after a day at the neighborhood swimming pool. I once even tried to sell trash, which didn't work out too well. That taught me even the best salesman can't sell a bad product!

In 1970 my dad accepted a call to Baytown, TX. Little did I know it would be that move which paved the way for my future in the newspaper business, although such a profession never entered my mind until my senior year in college.

## INTRODUCTION

My years in Baytown weren't all that unusual, I was all about sports, chasing girls, and hanging out in the great outdoors with my friends.

In high school I focused on basketball, which was my favorite sport, but only because a good friend and I both played quarterback at different junior high schools, and we didn't want to compete for the position in high school.

I spent many an hour playing basketball at the local YMCA. At some point in high school my dad pointed out I probably wouldn't reach my goal of playing in the NBA, and I might want to concentrate a little more on my studies. I was a solid "C" student at the time, but even at six foot, I could barely touch the net. I took my dad's advice and started paying a little more attention to the books.

Fred Hartman, the patriarch of the family I have worked for my entire career, was the editor and publisher of the *Baytown Sun* during much of the time I lived in Baytown.

In the fall of 1977 I entered Texas A&M University in College Station. I was a member of the Corps of Cadets, yet I was anything but military.

It was during my freshman year I learned about God's sense of humor. Out of nowhere, I physically matured, got faster, and could easily dunk a basketball.

While in the Corps, my outfit, Squadron 2, got a lot of recognition for athletic accomplishments in intramurals.

I won the high jump, and 100-yard and 220-yard-dashes in the Corps of Cadets intramural track championships a number of times.

Between my sophomore and junior years I attended Air Force summer camp at Lackland AFB in San Antonio. I decided against entering the Air Force upon graduation

# 30 YEARS THROUGH THE NEWS/LENS

when I was told I couldn't get a pilot's slot due to my eyesight. At 19, I decided I didn't want to give seven years of my life if I couldn't be "top dog" in the cockpit.

My last two years I focused on my studies, and served as executive officer of my outfit.

It was during my senior year I won an award in a Marketing and Media Planning competition. I worked alone on a project, instead of working with a team of students, because my professor said if I did well I would have a good chance of landing a position with a major advertising agency—my dream job.

I received several offers at the award ceremony, but turned them down when I received another offer during Christmas break my senior year.

The job was selling advertising at the *Brenham Banner-Press*, a daily newspaper in Brenham, TX.

I took that job because I was getting married and my fiancee was going to get her master's degree at Texas A&M.

The man who offered me that job had lived down the street in Baytown. He had been the advertising director for the *Baytown Sun*, but had since moved to Brenham as the assistant to the publisher.

A couple of weeks before I started my new job in Brenham, in 1981, my fiancee broke off the engagement and I was "stuck" in Brenham, single, and living with a retired couple because there was no place to rent due to the oil boom in the Giddings area.

I passed the time playing a lot of softball and basketball on league teams, and working hard at my new job.

I was promoted to advertising director after a little more than a year.

## INTRODUCTION

A short time later my boss and I drove to College Station to convince Dillard's to advertise in the *Banner-Press*.

The head of advertising for that particular store was a young lady named Diane Loria. She didn't say much that day during the "high level" meeting in the food court of Post Oak Mall.

A few months later, she called to place an advertisement. In the early 80s, however, one couldn't simply send an ad via email like it is done today. I had to drive to College Station, meet Diane, and then drive to the *Bryan Eagle* to pick it up. On that drive to the *Eagle*, Diane asked, "Do you have any job openings at the newspaper?"

It just so happened a position on the staff had opened up that morning, so I offered her the job.

Two weeks later she moved to Brenham, and for about 18 months I was her boss.

I became disillusioned with the newspaper business because it was no longer a challenge, and decided it was time to make a career change.

At about that time Diane asked me if I wanted to meet her and a couple of her friends at a dance hall in College Station.

She and I danced the night away...and shared our first kiss.

Sometime during that next week it was learned the editor and publisher of *The Rockport Pilot* had suffered an aneurysm the same night we went dancing.

Within a couple of weeks, Fred Hartman, who was now the owner of the *Brenham Banner-Press*, the same Fred

# 30 YEARS THROUGH THE NEWS/LENS

Hartman who had been the editor and publisher at the *Baytown Sun* when I lived in Baytown, told Charles Moser, the editor and publisher of the *Banner-Press*, he wanted to give me a shot at running one of his newspapers.

I left for Rockport in February 1984, and lived in an extra room in the home of the late Johnnie Vermillion until an apartment became available.

I was named editor and publisher when Bob Scott, the publisher who had the aneurysm, passed away. I was the youngest publisher in the Hartman family of newspapers at that time.

I have been involved in all aspects of community newspapering during my 33-year newspaper career, the last 30 of which have been as editor and publisher of the *Rockport Pilot*.

I have run the business, delivered newspapers, sold advertising, written numerous news stories, covered a lot of sports, penned a weekly column for 30 years, and shot a ton of pictures. If my camera isn't hanging from my neck, it's not far away.

I learned one of my most valuable lessons early in my career.

The first meeting I covered for the newspaper was a Rockport City Council meeting. One of the agenda items was a proposed strip annexation of property along the waterfront in one area of the county. It was very controversial at the time, and perhaps even illegal.

City Hall was packed with people I had never seen before.

When the meeting was over, many of those in attendance addressed me by name, said they subscribed to the newspaper, and told me they depended on the *Pilot* to give them the local news.

## INTRODUCTION

Family has always been very important in my life. This picture was taken in May 2014 in Las Vegas when our daughters were pregnant with our first grandchildren. I have pictures of my daughters "all dressed up" from most of our vacations. Here are, from left, Cody, Ashlee, Alyssa, Doug, Diane, and me.

It was at that exact moment I fully understood the residents of Aransas County—not "powerful" people in the community, close friends, or politicians—were my bosses, the people for whom I worked.

In my 30 years in Aransas County I have served on numerous boards, including the Rockport-Fulton Chamber of Commerce, Rockport Country Club, Rockport Rotary Club, North Bay Hospital in Aransas Pass, Aransas County EMS, The ACISD Education Foundation, Crime Stoppers of Aransas County, the Rockport-Fulton A&M Club, and the Texas Maritime Museum just to name a few.

# 30 YEARS THROUGH THE NEWS/LENS

I have been very blessed in my life, beginning with being born into a loving, Christian family.

Both of my parents are still active at 84 years of age.

A lot of water has gone under the bridge since I made landfall here in February 1984.

I got married to Diane Loria, who is currently the President/CEO of the Rockport-Fulton Chamber of Commerce, on Dec. 2, 1984.

We have two daughters—Alyssa, born in 1987, and Ashlee, born in 1989. After graduating from Rockport-Fulton High School, they earned their degrees at Texas A&M University, just like mom and dad.

In July 2010 Alyssa married Douglas Wilson (another Aggie).

In August 2013 Ashlee married Cody Lynch (another Aggie).

In 2014 both daughters and our sons-in-law brought grandsons into our lives.

Now that I'm done with this book, I'm going to settle back into my regular routine as newspaperman, and work on being a grandfather!

# 1984

## JANUARY

- Aransas County Emergency Medical Service (ACEMS) responded to 1,105 alarms in 1983. *3,716 calls were answered in 2013. The ACEMS ceased operations August 24, 2014 after almost 40 years of service to Aransas County (AC). The county, City of Rockport, and Town of Fulton signed contracts with Allegiance Ambulance for service effective August 24, 2014.*
- Allied Live Oak Bank opened. *Opened originally as Live Oak State Bank, it is now Prosperity Bank.*
- Harbor Oaks Village Shopping Village opened with Warehouse Foods as its anchor store. *ACE Hardware is now located in that space.*
- *The Magic Queen*, renamed *Wayward Lady* after breaking away from its moorings, was being built at Rockport Yacht and Supply Company (RYSCO). *The RYSCO property was located at the water's edge at the east end of Wharf Street.*
- The Paws & Taws Square Dance Building had been recently moved to its current location in Fulton Navigation Park. *Originally, it was built by square dancers on the property where the Lighthouse Inn is now located.*
- Bob Scott, *Rockport Pilot* (RP) Editor & Publisher, was diagnosed with an aneurism.

## FEBRUARY

- Mike Probst (MP) transferred to the *Rockport Pilot* (RP) from the *Brenham Banner-Press* to fill in for Bob Scott.

# 30 YEARS THROUGH THE NEWS/LENS

- Casting for the film *Alamo Bay* was announced. The film was about the struggles between shrimpers and Vietnamese shrimpers. *Ed Harris and Amy Madigan were cast in leading roles.*
- The new Rockport Post Office was opened on FM 2165 (Pearl Street). *Formerly located at Church and Market streets, it is still in use today. The AC Appraisal District is located in the old post office.*
- The O'Connor home was moved to its new location near Rockport Harbor to house The Rockport Center for the Arts (RCA). *The home's original location was across from the ski basin where a Valero gas station is now located.*
- Coastal Bend Hospital in Aransas Pass, the closest hospital to Rockport-Fulton, was sold to AMI. *The facility has been sold several times and is currently named Care Regional Medical Center.*
- The Aransas County Navigation District (ACND) approved the establishment of Veterans Memorial Park near Rockport Harbor.

**MARCH**

- The sale of Rockport Country Club (RCC) to Hasslocher Enterprises, Inc. was completed.
- James Michener visited Rockport and Fulton to gather information for his upcoming book, *Texas*.
- RP published its one and only *Progress Edition*.
- The Aransas County Independent School District (ACISD) enjoyed the use of a new auditorium, constructed with funds from a 1980 bond issue. It replaced one built at the high school in 1959. *Later renamed the Martha Luigi Auditorium in honor of the longtime Rockport-Fulton High School (RFHS) Choral Director, it continues to host community events and musical and dramatic programs.*

# 1984: YEAR ONE

- The new HEB store at Austin Street and Business SH 35, opening in 1983, was open 24 hours per day. *It is now a vacant building in downtown Rockport.*

## APRIL

- First responders trained for a growing Lamar community.
- A study for locating a hospital in AC was underway.
- MP wrote his first editorial on April 21 under the headline "Watchdog or Nuisance?" *It focused on irresponsible dog owners.*

## MAY

- Bob Scott, RP Editor & Publisher, died May 9, 1984.
- The capacity of the City of Rockport's wastewater treatment plant was doubled.
- Gladys Bruhl Gibson, the great-granddaughter of George Fulton, participated in the dedication and opening of the Fulton Mansion. This was the most expensive restoration project accomplished by the Texas Parks & Wildlife Department (TPWD).
- Capt. Ted Appell began guided bird tours on the MV Whooping Crane.

Gladys Gibson, the great-granddaughter of Col. George Ware Fulton, cuts the ribbon officially opening the Fulton Mansion to visitors.

# 30 YEARS THROUGH THE NEWS/LENS

MP's first photo in RP was this fatal accident, which claimed the life of Linda Schrenkeisen.

- The historical marker for Fulton Cemetery was dedicated.
- Linda Diana Schrenkeisen was killed in a fatal accident. *These accident photos were the first photos taken by MP for RP.*
- MP, 24, was named RP Editor & Publisher on May 30, 1984.

**JUNE**

- Estate lots at Rockport Country Club (RCC) went on sale.
- The layout of RP was changed to the new industry-wide six-column format.

**JULY**

- CP&L opened its new office at Highway 35 and Ann Street. *Value Bank is now located there.*
- MP wrote his first personal column for the RP under the headline "Prostitutes & Taxes." *MP continues to write a weekly column.*
- Support was sought for dredging Cedar Bayou. The nonprofit organization, *Save Cedar Bayou*, was formed. *The bayou was dredged several times since 1984, the most recent dredging taking place in 2014.*
- Brush at Memorial Park was cleared and playground equipment was installed.

# 1984: YEAR ONE

- Aubrey Schulz was hired as RFHS head football coach.
- Walmart had an all-weather tire advertised for $32.97. *All weather tires at Walmart now range between $63 and $119.*

## AUGUST

- A Paramedic Support and Training Center opened. *The Little Old Ladies in Tennis Shoes sold homemade crafts in their boutique, located in the building, to raise money for the ACEMS. The building is now available for lease.*
- The ACISD adjusted operations in the wake of House Bill 72. Because the ACISD is deemed a "wealthy" school district, even though a majority of the students are economically disadvantaged, the State of Texas distributes local school tax revenue to underfunded districts. *School funding continues to be a prominent issue in Texas.*
- A new pavilion was built at Memorial Park.
- The Laguna Reef Hotel's owners asked the City of Rockport's Planning & Zoning Commission (P&Z) to allow them to build

*The Little Old Ladies in Tennis Shoes* opened the Paramedic Support Center and then went back to work making handmade crafts to support the ACEMS.

# 30 YEARS THROUGH THE NEWS/LENS

the hotel taller than height restrictions allowed. *The P&Z did not make exceptions to the restrictions. Due to that decision, the owners built the hotel as planned with four floors, but the structure has a low ceiling in the lobby.*

**SEPTEMBER**

- The Rockport City Council approved a three percent Hotel Occupancy Tax (HOT). *By 2014, the City of Rockport, Town of Fulton, and AC were charging a seven percent HOT.*
- Users of the festival grounds and the ACND fought over user fees.
- The ACISD tax rate was $.6850, and the AC tax rate was $.29. *The 2013 tax rates were: ACISD, $1.16049; AC, $.375276; ACND, $.055136; City of Rockport, $.327728; and Town of Fulton, $.2503.*
- An editorial in RP supported the idea that HOT funds should be committed to the Rockport-Fulton Chamber of Commerce (RFCC) to promote all of AC. *The Chamber was called the Rockport Area Chamber of Commerce in 1984. This was six years prior*

RFJHS students worked on new TRS-80 Radio Shack computers in the school's new computer lab.

# 1984: YEAR ONE

*to Diane, MP's wife, being hired as the RFCC's Executive Director.*
- A fundraising drive was launched for the proposed Texas Maritime Museum (TMM). *Additional fund-raising events continue to be held including the Wine Festival, Mahjong Tournament, and the Belle Ball.*
- The Rockport-Fulton Tourist Development Group was formed.
- The state began charging sales tax on newspapers.

When the Texas Maritime Museum Fund Drive kicked off, an anchor was placed at the site of the future museum at Rockport Harbor.

## OCTOBER

- The 10th Annual Seafair was held.
- The Town of Fulton broke ground on a $36,000 hike and bike trail with pavilion.
- The City of Rockport began planning for a new city hall and purchased land from Chester Johnson for $120,000. *The RFCC and Visitor's Center is now located at the site of the old City Hall.*
- The 3,000-acre Bakers Port Project was proposed for AC. *This project failed to materialize.*
- The possible construction of a desalinization plant was studied.

# 30 YEARS THROUGH THE NEWS/LENS

- Seventy-five percent of AC's registered voters cast votes in the election, which featured Walter Mondale and Ronald Reagan on the ticket.
- A story focusing on the harmful effects of pollution and its effects might have on Whooping Cranes was published. *Whooping Cranes are still recognized as an endangered species.*

## NOVEMBER

- New flood maps used to determine insurance rates were proposed.
- The Association of Progressive and Orderly Growth was formed.
- ACISD Trustees studied the possibility of building a new high school.
- Demus Troy Casterline was arrested on charges of murder and sexual assault.
- Eighty-three Whooping Cranes were counted at the Aransas National Wildlife Refuge (ANWR). *U.S. Fish & Wildlife Biologists estimated a population of 250 Whooping Cranes in 2014.*

## DECEMBER

- Stewart Title opened.
- Rockport Bank opened. *It later became Bank of Corpus Christi and then IBC Bank. It was relocated in a new building at the intersection of State Highway 35 (SH 35) and Traylor Boulevard.*
- The wedding announcement of MP, and Diane, his wife, was published in the December 29 edition. They were married on December 2.

# 1985

## JANUARY

- The consolidation of tax collecting among the governing entities was discussed.
- A study reported that the 300,000 people, who annually visit AC, have a $50 million impact on the local economy.
- The name of the pier at Fulton Navigation Park was changed from Casterline Pier to Fulton Pier.
- MP wrote a column under the headline, "Married Life is Great."
- Pat Blair, RP managing editor, left the newspaper and moved to Wyoming.
- A new public library building was explored.
- Plans for the new Oaks Office Park were approved.

## FEBRUARY

- The shrimping industry suffered under stifling insurance costs. Insurance premiums for Jackson Seafood Company doubled.
- The new clubhouse at RCC opened.
- Henry Bickerstaff was hired as RP Managing Editor.
- The Courtyard Apartments were built.
- A large brush fire burned more than 300 acres. Ten neighboring fire departments helped fight the flames.
- The City of Rockport annexed 109 acres, which included RCC Estates.

# 30 YEARS THROUGH THE NEWS/LENS

- First Baptist Church expanded its downtown location.
- The Rockport Sail Club built a new clubhouse.
- Papagayo Restaurant opened on SH 35 N. *Copano Bay Café can now be found at that location.*
- MP wrote a column about his grandmother's 80th birthday.

## MARCH

- A bond election for Rockport's new city hall was approved with a 138 to 76 vote.
- After receiving a bomb threat, Rockport Police Department (RPD) officers discovered two small cans filled with gunpowder under Gene's Lounge in downtown Rockport. *That location is now Rowdy Maui.*
- Security Real Estate merged with Palm Harbor Real Estate.
- L.E. Casterline won the oyster shucking championship at the 6th Annual Fulton Oysterfest for the sixth year in a row.
- Rockport Mayor C.H. "Burt" Mills was charged with DWI.
- Demus Troy Casterline filed suit against an AC Sheriff's deputy for mental distress. Casterline was being treated in a hospital at the time.
- The Rockport City Council began planning for a new police station and fire substation.
- The City of Rockport's wastewater treatment plant was expanded.

## APRIL

- Demus Troy Casterline was set free on bail.
- New playground equipment was installed at Memorial Park.
- Controversy began regarding the electrical job at Rockport Harbor.

- Sen. Phil Gramm spoke at the annual RFCC banquet.
- Ray O'Brien was elected mayor of Rockport.
- MP wrote a column about the upcoming decision regarding the location of the new Navy Homeport.
- The film, *Alamo Bay*, was released. Local residents who appeared in the film included Carolyn Farnsworth, Le Nguyen, Ed and Barbara Opstad, Tuan Tran, Chris Blum, Lan Ti Do, Laura Casterline, Zuan Thi Le, Donna Nugent, Howard McNutt, Tim Gillis, Dat Nguyen, and David Ivanoski. Adult movie tickets were $3.50.
- The Sorenson home was moved to Orleans Street.

## MAY

- Ground was broken for the Sorenson Place Condominiums on Water Street.
- A study focused on the possibility of Fulton residents connecting to City of Rockport Utilities.
- The Fulton Harbor pavilion neared completion.
- The *AC Crop Hunger Walk* drew about 100 people.
- A RP editorial ran under the headline "AC Facing Big Decision on $17 million School Bond Issue."
- The school bond issue was voted down 1,365 to 406 votes.
- Footworks Dance Studio opened.
- The Oak Bay Condominiums were under construction by Willard R. Baker.
- The local chamber changed its name to the Rockport-Fulton Area Chamber of Commerce.
- A woman reported seeing a UFO twice the size of a streetlight.

# 30 YEARS THROUGH THE NEWS/LENS

## JUNE

- Gene Garcia served as defense attorney for Demus Troy Casterline
- Gene Johnson was hired as manager of the AC Airport.
- Demus Troy Casterline was found guilty and sentenced to life in prison.
- Bruce Stark proposed building a Best Western in Fulton.
- The Smith home, owned by RYSCO's T. Noah Smith, was remodeled. *This house is now known as the Hoopes-Smith House, a bed and breakfast.*

## JULY

- Officials announced the location of the new Navy Homeport would be in Ingleside.
- Seaside Development was proposed in Lamar.
- The City of Rockport and the Town of Fulton presented their first HOT checks to the RFCC.

Fulton Mayor Les "Googles" Cole presents the Town's first HOT check to the RFCC's John Jackson and Bill Mayhood.

Rockport Mayor C.H. "Burt" Mills presents the City's first HOT check to the RFCC's Gayna Harrel.

# 1985: YEAR TWO

- The City of Rockport's three parks received improvements.
- The Fulton Town Council decided to build its own wastewater treatment plant. *The treatment plant was never built.*
- New traffic signals were installed on SH 35 at Pearl (FM 2165) and Live Oak Streets.
- Ground was broken on Rockport's new city hall on Market Street. *It is still in use today.*

## AUGUST

- Ground was broken on the new Rockport Police Station.

Ground is broken on the RPD's new station. That station made way for the current Public Safety Center and is no longer in existence.

- Sipe Real Estate ran the largest real estate advertisement in RP. *In 2014, the Sipe Real Estate building was demolished to make way for a new convenience store.*
- Rental Equipment Center opened.
- With the aid of HOT funds, the RFCC board approved an advertising proposal with Pettus Advertising.

# 30 YEARS THROUGH THE NEWS/LENS

## SEPTEMBER

- Rockport Mayor C.H. "Burt" Mills was sentenced to three days in jail for his DWI.
- First National Bank's Town Hall was made available for meetings. *The building has since been demolished.*
- MP wrote his first story under his byline, which focused on the Seafair Committee discussing insurance needs.
- Lewis Cass, motion picture pioneer, visited Capt. Harry Sloat and Dori, his wife.
- Marry Harrist won $25,000 in a cable television contest.
- Sacred Heart School added two additional classrooms.
- ACND employees received new uniforms.
- Wayne Lindsey's boat was destroyed by fire off the shoreline of Key Allegro.
- AC received a $92,000 medical bill for Demus Troy Casterline's hospital stay, which AC denied paying.
- New sidewalks were installed at Rockport Harbor.

## OCTOBER

- Michael Meek was named special projects manager at Security Real Estate. *He is currently the president/CEO of the Greater New Braunfels Chamber of Commerce.*
- Pawelek Meats opened.
- Ben Crenshaw, professional golfer, visited RCC during the Member-Guest Tournament.
- The Tenneco Oil Gas Processing Plant terminated production in Lamar.
- Paul Grohman was hired as Rockport's City Manager.
- Construction began on restrooms at Fulton Harbor.

MP was the chairman of the Seafair Crab Races for a few years after moving to Rockport. When the RFCC took over Seafair in 2000, he agreed to handle the races once again.

- An oil buildup forced the closure of Fulton Harbor.
- Federal Wallop-Breaux Funds were released to fund the first Cedar Bayou Dredging Project.
- Eduardo Romero and Steve Veriate, professional golfers, played in a PGA qualifying school tournament at RCC.
- KPLAY, AC's new FM radio station, went on the air.

**NOVEMBER**

- Carquest Auto Parts opened.
- A new Youth Support Center opened.
- The United Way of AC raised just under $40,000.
- MP wrote a column entitled "Leave Social Security Alone."

# 30 YEARS THROUGH THE NEWS/LENS

**DECEMBER**

- Construction on Kontiki Beach Condos was completed.
- James H. Sorenson was named chairman of the board of First National Bank, while Bob Mosier was named president. *First National Bank is now Wells Fargo Bank.*
- Due to rising insurance costs and lower market prices, local shrimpers did not have a good year.

## JANUARY

- A study was made regarding the effect of the AC Municipal Utility District's effluent release on oysters from its Lamar treatment plant.
- The Copano Bay Villas were opened in Cape Velero.

## FEBRUARY

- RFHS began its soccer program.
- MP wrote a column about the experience of sitting next to Mary Lou Retton, Olympic gold medal gymnast, during a banquet in Houston.
- Leggett Light Channel was dredged.
- Phil Blackmar, 28, was hired as the touring golf pro at RCC.
- AC Commissioners began discussions about operating under a Unit Road System.
- The first home in Cape Velero was toured.
- The former Rockport City Hall on Austin Street was sold to John Wall for $125,500.

## MARCH

- C.H. "Burt" Mills, Mayor of Rockport, established the *Rockport Tomorrow Task Force*.
- RP published its *Texas Sesquicentennial Edition*.
- ACISD trustees proposed a $5.5 million Bond Issue.
- The Town of Fulton formed a municipal court.

# 30 YEARS THROUGH THE NEWS/LENS

- A ribbon cutting was held for Hugh's IGA. *Bealls is now at that location.*

**APRIL**

- Willard Baker proposed building a mini-mall at Austin and St. Mary's Streets called Austin Street Station. *The building was previously Roe's Food Store.*
- MP wrote a column under the headline, "Terrorism: Will It Ever End?"
- An open house was held at the old Fulton School, marking its 100th Birthday.
- The RFHS Band played at a rally in support of the school bond issue.
- The new Rockport City Hall on Market Street opened.

The ribbon cutting for Rockport City Hall was a big event. The building is still used by the City.

# 1986: YEAR THREE

## MAY

- The Winnebago Owners Convention was held in Rockport attracting 250 members.
- MP wrote an article describing an upcoming bus trip. Thirty-eight community leaders learned about park systems along the coast. This was the impetus, which led to the $500,000 Texas Parks and Wildlife Department (TPWD) matching grant, used to develop the Rockport Beach Park and build the pavilions.
- The formation of a Parks Board was discussed.
- It was announced Seafair would be held in downtown Rockport, rather than on the festival grounds.
- The Stella Maris Chapel was moved to its new home across from the Lamar Cemetery.
- AC voters turned down the proposed school bonds.
- ACISD trustees voted to try the Bond Election again on July 12.
- Paul Grohman, Rockport City Manager, received a contract guaranteeing a severance package, if fired.

## JUNE

- The new downtown mini-mall located at St. Mary and Austin Streets opened. *Different types of shops currently serve customers there.*
- A *Beach Task Force* was formed to study future development of Rockport Beach.
- Plans for Rockport Beach were shared at a packed meeting at Rockport City Hall.

## JULY

- RP received first place in column writing from the Texas Press Association.

# 30 YEARS THROUGH THE NEWS/LENS

- A woman left a two-year-old child in her car. The child drove the car into the bay.
- Seven people were injured during the Wendell Family Fireworks Display when the fireworks exploded prematurely.
- Val Hunter, RFHS student, was shot and killed on Rockport Beach.
- The school bond election failed again with 1,012 votes for and 1,195 against.
- Officials began computerizing the tax system.
- *Renaissance '86*, a planning tool for Rockport's future, was established.
- A curfew was set at Rockport beach after the death of Val Hunter. *The entrance to Rockport beach is now closed at midnight.*
- Rockport's unemployment rate was 12 percent.

A new curfew was enforced at Rockport Beach after RFHS student Val Hunter was shot and killed.

# 1986: YEAR THREE

## AUGUST
- The RFCC adopted its first *Program of Work. It continues to produce one each year.*
- A group was formed to fund 400 street signs needed for the County Street Project.
- The Rockport-Fulton Consumer Association was formed. Those shopping locally received a 10 percent discount at selected businesses.
- Issac "Shorty" Garcia, a local shrimper, drowned in Fulton Harbor when his boat capsized.
- The Fulton Town Council approved raising the HOT rate by one cent.

## SEPTEMBER
- John Roberts, RFHS senior, was held hostage in an attempted robbery at Price Lo Grocery in the Harbor Oaks Village Shopping Center.
- The City of Rockport raised its HOT tax from three to six cents. Of that, four cents was given to the RFCC to use for promoting AC.
- Estelle Stair was the Seafair Poster Artist.
- Elouise Boling State Farm Insurance opened in Rockport's old city hall building. *The RFCC is now located there.*

## OCTOBER
- A 24-foot section of bulkhead on north beach collapsed.
- A methamphetamine operation located at 20 Flamingo on Key Allegro was busted.

## NOVEMBER
- Sewer became a subject of debate in discussions about the annexation of Key Allegro.

# 30 YEARS THROUGH THE NEWS/LENS

- Mark White, Governor, and Henry Cisneros, San Antonio Mayor, landed at the AC Airport. They were on their way to Ingleside for a Homeport event.
- John Wendell, incumbent AC Judge, beat Max Kluge for the judge's post.
- A total of $20,000 was spent to thwart negative publicity regarding a red tide outbreak.
- *Fish Fest* was held to fight negative red tide publicity.
- *A Renaissance '86* public forum was held.
- The Texas Department of Transportation (TxDOT) placed the SH 35 bypass in its 10-year plan. *Numerous fatal accidents occurred after the first phase was completed and while the highway was an undivided two-lane roadway. The 4-lane divided highway has since been completed.*
- ACISD trustees approved the construction of a new gym at Rockport-Fulton Junior High School (RFJHS).
- ACND Commissioners approved the development of Cove Harbor North.

The RFCC held a *Nostalgia Night* at the old Dallas Night Club in the Harbor Oaks Village Shopping Center, now the site of Cinema 4.

**DECEMBER**

- Fulton Elementary School was connected to the Rockport Sanitary Sewer System.
- MP wrote a column under the headline, "Is Government Getting Too Big?"
- The ACISD purchased 42 acres near the intersection of FM 2165 and FM 1781 for $4,900 per acre.

# 1987

## JANUARY

- The Rockport City Council adopted a flood insurance ordinance.
- The TPWD awarded the City of Rockport a $750,000 matching grant for the development of Rockport Beach Park.
- Hal Bassett was hired as the RFCC's first Executive Director.
- AC proposed adding a half-cent sales tax to be used for indigent health care and related expenses.

The Renaissance Idea Fair brought community members together to develop a vision for AC's future.

# 30 YEARS THROUGH THE NEWS/LENS

- An escapee from the AC Jail was apprehended.
- AC Commissioners selected an architect for the new AC Library.
- The City of Rockport and the ACND determined details of an agreement for the operation of the Rockport Beach Park. *The City operated the Park for 25 years. During that time the ACND paid the City $25,000 per year as long as beach operated at a loss. In May 2012, the ACND took control of that asset.*

## FEBRUARY

- MP wrote a column about the burglary of his home.
- Steve Kennedy, TPWD Game Warden, began writing his outdoor column in RP.
- Bryan Bracht of Bracht Lumber Company built a china cabinet for the RFCC's Annual Chinese Auction.
- Members of the Audubon Society were passengers on the first trip of the *MV Skimmer*.
- Bruce Wallace was hired as AC's first Unit Road Administrator.
- The ACND filed for a Beach Restoration Bond Election.
- A new dispatch system went live. New phone numbers were assigned to the Aransas County Sheriff's Office (ACSO) 729-2222, and the RPD, 729-1111.

## MARCH

- Street signs built by the RFHS Vocational Education Department were installed.

## APRIL

- A 30,000-square-foot addition was approved for Fulton Elementary.

# 1987: YEAR FOUR

- AC's proposed half-cent sales tax was placed on the ballot.
- The RFCC approved hiring its first advertising agency.
- Marijuana was found being harvested at the Alligator Camp on Business SH 35.
- Jerry Brundrett resigned as President of the ACISD board of trustees. Annabelle Henry was named President.
- Charles Augustine, ACND Chairman, signed the Intergovernmental Agreement for the operation of Rockport Beach Park.
- Charles Augustine, ACND Chairman, suffered severe burns in an explosion at Bart's RV Park where he was employed. He died on April 27.
- Rockport-Fulton Real Estate opened.

## MAY

- The RFCC approved a $100,000 advertising plan to promote Rockport-Fulton.
- The bond issue to refurbish Rockport Beach was approved with 768 votes for and 617 against. The vote to refurbish Rockport Beach and build a deep-water marina failed to pass. *The marina was proposed in the area south of the jetty and at the south end of Rockport Beach.*
- Downtown merchants learned about the *Main Street Program*.
- House and Senate resolutions designated Rockport the official site of the TMM.
- The *Rockport-Fulton Area Economic Development Corporation* was incorporated.

## JUNE

- Permit problems postponed the Beach Restoration Project.

# 30 YEARS THROUGH THE NEWS/LENS

- ❑ The RFCC changed its logo from the "drinking fish" and *Toast of the Coast* to *The Charm of the Texas Coast.*

**JULY**

- ❑ RP published its first special section for the RFCC's Annual Banquet. MP served as RFCC Vice-President at that time.
- ❑ AC Commissioners dismissed Bruce Wallace, Unit Road Administrator, for inappropriate moving of county equipment. He had been employed at this position for five months.
- ❑ A one-year in-county subscription to RP was $20.

Property owners were in an uproar about property appraisals. The owner of this trailer said it was appraised at $15,000, even though he only paid $1,500 for it.

- ❑ After six months, Hal Bassett, RFCC's first Executive Director, resigned for personal reasons.
- ❑ Paul Grohman, Rockport's City Manager, was investigated regarding his role with drug funds, while serving as city manager in Denver City.

# 1987: YEAR FOUR

Children's movies were a staple at the old Cinema 35. This photo made some people upset because they thought the kids were watching the R-rated *The Witches of Eastwick*, which was the regular show posted on the marquee.

## AUGUST

- ❏ The largest number of property owners to attend a public hearing in Rockport packed City Hall. The City Council proposed annexing 620 acres along the shoreline of Copano Bay.
- ❏ Tad Jarrett, AC Appraisal District Chief Appraiser, was dismissed.
- ❏ MP wrote a column about his Opa (grandfather) passing away. His next column focused on Lamaze classes since his first daughter was due in September.
- ❏ MP wrote his first Rockport City Council story for the August 29 edition. The subject was the City of Rockport's attempt to annex property along Copano Bay.

# 30 YEARS THROUGH THE NEWS/LENS

## SEPTEMBER

- Red Athey was hired as AC's new road administrator.
- Fulton raised its HOT rate to six cents.
- AC Catholics boarded buses for San Antonio to see Pope John Paul II in San Antonio.
- MP wrote a column under the headline "It's a Girl!" about the birth of his first child. An accompanying column, under the headline "And now the facts of the situation" was *written* by his daughter.
- The Navy began using the AC Airport for pilot training.

It was a big day when the dredging of Cedar Bayou pushed through to the Gulf of Mexico.

## OCTOBER

- Paul Kirtley was offered the job as the RFCC's new Executive Director. He did not take the job.
- Tommy Moon, president of Vermillion Construction Co., Larry Heser, superintendent, and Mark Perry, equipment operator, were killed in a plane crash in Refugio County. On their way to Corsicana, Texas for a final inspection of a project, the plane's engine malfunctioned and all perished in the accident. *Vermillion Construction built seawalls, streets, roads and laid sewer and water lines for many canal subdivisions along the Texas coast including Key Allegro, Bahia Bay and Harbor Oaks. Vermillion Construction continued operations until November 1989 when it closed its doors after 28 years.*

## 1987: YEAR FOUR

- The playground equipment at Memorial Park was removed after it was deemed unsafe.

The RFCC's public mural program began with a mural on the old State Farm Building. That structure, which was originally Rockport City Hall, is now part of the RFCC's offices and Visitor's Center.

- The RFCC began work on its mural program. Elouise Boling's State Farm office received the first mural.
- Work began on the $1.5 million Rockport Beach Renovation Project.

### NOVEMBER

- Bob Lynch was hired as the RFCC's new executive director.
- According to the ANWR, Whooping Cranes numbered 116 birds.

### DECEMBER

- RP published its first Visitor's Guide. The RFCC designated it as the *Official Guide*. The next *Visitor's Guide* was published by *The Herald*; however, it was printed late. MP told the RFCC the RP would publish the *Visitor's Guide* twice per year regardless of whether the RFCC referred to it as its official *Visitor's Guide. Currently, the Visitor's Guide is published*

# 30 YEARS THROUGH THE NEWS/LENS

*annually in April and October. Now called the "Guide to Aransas County," it is the most comprehensive publication promoting AC and local businesses.*

- ❏ Eddie James Johnson was indicted for killing David Magee, Virginia Cadena, and her daughter Elizabeth Galvan.
- ❏ Work was underway on the north and south groins, which would frame the new Rockport Beach Park.
- ❏ Plans were made to hold the *National Collegiate Sports Festival* at Rockport beach, and other locations in AC.

# 1988: YEAR FIVE

## JANUARY

- RP offered free spot color with the purchase of a full-page advertisement.
- The Rockport-Fulton Tourist Association merged with the Rockport-Fulton Motel/Condo Association.
- Todd Hunter, running as a Democrat, sought state office.
- The new *Welcome to Rockport-Fulton* and *Thank You for Visiting Rockport-Fulton* signs were in place.
- Estelle Stair died at the age of 77.
- Richard Dias Construction built the Texas Maritime Museum's (TMM) new office. Rich Tillman, Marine Extension Agent, was housed there.
- The initial bids for the Rockport Beach Park improvements were over budget.
- Don Hanks was named president of Rockport Bank.
- Rockport Seafair moved back to the festival grounds after its one-year experience holding the event in downtown Rockport.
- The final *Renaissance '86* Report was released. *The Renaissance '86 report served as a guide for future growth in AC.*
- The *National Collegiate Sports Festival* to be held in Rockport was rejected due to action taken by RCC regarding the use of its facilities.

# 30 YEARS THROUGH THE NEWS/LENS

## FEBRUARY

- Allied Bank was purchased by First Interstate Bank.
- The Stella Maris Chapel was dedicated at its new site near the Lamar Cemetery.
- The Beach Park Gift Catalog, seeking items for the new park, was distributed.

Shrimpers were not pleased when told they had to start using Turtle Excluder Devices (TEDs).

- Shrimpers were required to use Turtle Excluder Devices (TEDs).
- Motorists pulled onto the shoulder of the highway across from the AC airport to watch the Navy's inaugural "touch & go" practice. *The Navy continues to use the airport for that purpose today.*
- Susie Bracht Black (then Stephens) and Katie Bickham became the first female members of the Rockport Rotary Club.
- Ground was broken on Homeport, Naval Station Ingleside. The *U.S.S. Lexington* sailed to the location for the event. *The U.S.S. Lexington is now a museum and has been permanently berthed at North Beach in Corpus Christi.*

# 1988: YEAR FIVE

- A pile driver was on site preparing for the construction of the beach pavilions at Rockport Beach Park.
- The first phase of the TMM was approved.
- RP published a special section about the Homeport Groundbreaking. *To this day, it is the only special section published by RP about a topic outside AC.*

## MARCH

- The Boiling Pot won best dish at the *Taste of Rockport-Fulton*.
- L.E. Casterline won the $1,000 raffle at the RFCC Chinese Auction.
- *Good Morning Vietnam* was showing at the local theater.
- Charter Savings opened.
- A mural called *The Children's Wall* was painted on the west wall of SeaAire Shopping Center. *The mural has since been painted over.*

The Children's Wall on the west side of the SeaAire Shopping Center involved many area children in painting the mural.

# 30 YEARS THROUGH THE NEWS/LENS

- The Rockport City Council tabled action regarding its 911 Emergency Service Ordinance.
- RP raised its newsstand price to 35 cents.

**APRIL**

- The RFCC opposed a proposed $50,000 Homestead Exemption.
- A group of 40 bankers met for a conference at the new Laguna Reef Hotel.
- Paul Grohman, Rockport City Manager, resigned. He accepted a similar position in New Braunfels. *He is now working as a realtor in Houston.*
- The new Burger King was under construction. *It is now Panda Bay restaurant.*
- Eddie James Johnson was convicted of capital murder and was sentenced to death.
- More than 230 people joined the Just Say No Club.

James H. Sorenson Jr. announced at a press conference funding was in place to begin the first phase of the TMM.

## 1988: YEAR FIVE

- Five entities signed a resolution opposing a proposed $50,000 Homestead Exemption.
- A group of elected officials and interested residents toured community pools around the area.
- More than 200 million Redfish fry were released in Aransas Bay.
- MP wrote a column about the *Shoot the Hoop Basketball Tournament* and alleged he was getting old. *At that time, he was 29 years old and his RFCC team won first place.*
- Construction on the first phase of the TMM was announced.

**MAY**

- Charlie Bright, ACISD Superintendent, resigned.
- A historical marker for the Fulton Mansion was dedicated.
- L.E. Casterline ran against C.H. "Burt" Mills, incumbent Rockport Mayor. *Mills won the mayoral election.*
- The $50,000 Homestead Exemption proposal failed.
- An incident involving a new RVFD fire truck and Rockport Mayor C.H. "Burt" Mills was investigated. Mills released information about the incident.
- Victoria's Gold & Gems held its grand opening.
- MP wrote a column about the difficult decision officials faced regarding the operation of Rockport Beach Park.
- Work to clear the rights of way for the new SH 35 bypass was underway.
- The Pilot House Restaurant was destroyed by fire.
- Rockport Beach Park parking permits went on sale for $10 (annual) and $2 (daily). *The fees today are $15 (annual) and $5 (daily).*

# 30 YEARS THROUGH THE NEWS/LENS

- The Rockport Beach Park entrance booth was built.
- C.H. "Burt" Mills, Rockport Mayor, resigned.
- Employees of the Duck Inn Restaurant, which C.H. "Burt" Mills owned, wrote a letter expressing support for him.
- Danny Adams was appointed Rockport's new mayor.
- Garry Mauro, Texas General Land Office Commissioner, was the keynote speaker at the RFCC Annual Banquet.

**JUNE**

- Asbestos was removed from RFJHS.
- Richard Holt was hired as TMM's first Executive Director.
- The new AC Library opened.
- The Coastal Bend Council of Governments reported AC was the fastest growing county in the region.
- Karen Hall was named ACISD Superintendent.
- The first fatal accident of the year involved a motorcycle and a car and occurred at the intersection of Business SH 35 and Colorado Street.

**JULY**

- MP wrote a column about camping at Guadalupe State Park for the first time with a daughter, who was less than one year old. The next week he wrote about trying to quit dipping tobacco with the help of hypnosis. *Probst no longer dips, but chews a cigar!*

**AUGUST**

- Lucille Hinson, Fulton City Secretary, resigned.
- *A Summer Celebration* marked the opening of the new beach. *The Beach Park has since earned the status of being Texas' first Blue Wave Beach and is one of only four on the Texas Coast with that designation.*

## 1988: YEAR FIVE

- Radio Shack opened in Live Oak Shopping Center. It is now located in Harbor Oaks Village Shopping Center.

Rockport Beach Park was finally opened to the public.

- MP wrote a column about his 10-year high school reunion.
- An erosion problem on Key Allegro was investigated.
- Rockport was listed among the best-rated retirement cities and towns in Consumer Guide.
- The TPWD cracked down on illegal netting.

### SEPTEMBER

- A 12-year-old boy riding a bicycle was killed when a car struck him.
- Hurricane Gilbert, the largest hurricane in history at that time, threatened the area. Local officials called for an evacuation. The storm, which reached Category 5 status, eventually made landfall in Mexico.
- Garry Mauro, Texas General Land Commissioner, honored Lola L. Bonner, a local attorney.

# 30 YEARS THROUGH THE NEWS/LENS

## OCTOBER

- Crime Stoppers of AC was organized.
- Rob Robison was named Rockport's new City Manager.
- The ANWR celebrated its 40th Anniversary.

## NOVEMBER

- Roy Rogero, former owner of the RP, died at the age of 80.
- A historical marker for Rockport Cemetery was unveiled.
- MP wrote a column about Blue Bell Ice Cream coming to the Corpus Christi area. *In 1981, MP began his newspaper career in Brenham, the home of Blue Bell Ice Cream.*
- A rededication ceremony was held at Sacred Heart Church after it was expanded by approximately 200 seats.

## DECEMBER

- The RFCC held a *Welcome Winter Texan Pancake Supper.*
- The Community Choir performed in concert.
- The TMM's Newsletter, *The Log Line, Volume 1, Number 1,* was inserted in RP.
- Joe Hinojosa, RPD chief, was suspended after patrolman Jerry Lawing claimed sexual harassment of male employees.

The RFCC began promoting AC using HOT funds for billboards and related media. This billboard was located on the outskirts of Sinton.

**1988: YEAR FIVE**

- The (anti-drug) PRIDE group was established.
- The Heldenfels donated land for a park at Tiger Field.
- Norman Scott and John Uhr were named directors at First National Bank.
- The first billboard promoting the Rockport-Fulton area was erected at the intersection of Highway 181 and FM 881.
- A new hangar was completed at the AC Airport.

# 30 YEARS THROUGH THE NEWS/LENS

## JANUARY

- A Whooping Crane was shot from a blind by a hunter. Capt. Ted Appel held a memorial service.
- A RVFD fire truck rolled over on the wet roadway at the sharp curve on Liberty Street (Business SH 35 S.) en route to a fire. Fireman Thomas DePuma walked away with no injuries.
- *Inc.* magazine named Coastal Productions as one of the fastest growing private companies in America.
- Watersedge RV Park opened.
- The expansion and renovations of First Presbyterian Church were dedicated.
- John Wendell, AC Judge, suggested having two Justices of the Peace instead of four.

## FEBRUARY

- MP wrote a column about his parents retiring.
- Waffle Cone Company opened.
- A deadly mushroom (*amanita pseudoverna*) was found at the ANWR.
- MP wrote a column under the headline "The Waiting Game," about the multiple false alarms Diane, his wife, had awaiting the birth of his second daughter. The next week his column was about her birth.
- Tucker Rackley, RFHS athletic director and head football coach, resigned.

# 1989: YEAR SIX

- Chris Brock, RPD Patrolman, spoke out in support of Joe Hinojosa, RPD chief.

## MARCH

- Jerry Moore and Andy Hall were hired to run the TMM.
- TxDOT announced the SH 35 bypass would extend to FM 3036.
- The Charter Food Store awning fell following a storm. *That store is no longer in existence. It was purchased and demolished by Camper Clinic for use as sales lot.*
- Wimpy Wright's Shrimp Boat was donated to the TMM.
- Rockport-Fulton sailors competed in San Francisco on *Blue Bayou II*.
- Ryan Dias was selected to play golf in *Australia Sport for Understanding Golf*.

## APRIL

- MP wrote a column about his daughter being baptized by his father on his father's last Sunday as a parish minister.
- Law enforcement officials made a heroin bust that had a street value of $4 million.
- A group of AC residents went to Austin to discuss windstorm insurance rates with State Rep. Todd Hunter.
- Rusty Hamilton was hired as RFHS' new athletic director and head football coach.
- A local birder's guide for the Rockport-Fulton area was made available at the RFCC.
- The Fulton Town Council approved a $1 surcharge on utility bills to help fund Fulton Volunteer Fire Department (FVFD) operations.

# 30 YEARS THROUGH THE NEWS/LENS

- The newly-organized AC Humane Society accepted a check from Lisa Guillett.
- L.E. Casterline, Oyster Shucking National Champion, was honored by the Texas House of Representatives.
- The Baumgart Water Company in Holiday Beach was sold to the Holiday Beach Utility Company.
- Rose Smith was named ACISD School Board President.

**MAY**

- The ACND offered 10 cents per square foot for property in front of Cove Harbor.
- The mural on A Blossom Shop was completed.
- The RFCC announced a new brochure would promote the Rockport Beach Park.
- The Economic Development Corporation looked at the feasibility of a community/facility center.
- The TMM received a donation of a portable oil platform.
- A bill in the House of Representatives benefitting the ACND was approved. The law allowed for a promotion and development fund for ACND properties.
- Gussie Deane, AC Auditor, retired.
- A man was stabbed four times at Rockport Beach Park.
- The Bay Area Olympics was slated for the Rockport Beach Park.
- Rockport Beach Park parking permit sales in one weekend totaled 1,403 daily permits and 233 annual permits.
- The inaugural *Celebration of Lights* was planned for the Rockport Beach Park and downtown Rockport. The goal was to light up downtown Rockport.

# 1989: YEAR SIX

## JUNE

- The inaugural *Bob Lilly Whooping Crane 10K Run* was planned.
- Tim Jayroe of Tyler was hired as the new RPD chief.
- Father Gregory Deane was honored by Sacred Heart Catholic Church for his 35 years of service to the Diocese.
- Jason Mills was nominated to the U.S. Air Force Academy by Congressman Greg Laughlin.
- Will McDonald, Pat McDonald, and Darnell Schreiber were named new principals at ACISD campuses.
- MP wrote a column about the death of Nana, his wife's grandmother.
- The first four-way stop signs were installed in RCC.
- James H. Sorenson was elected Chairman of the Board of the TMM.
- First Presbyterian Church celebrated its centennial.
- Susie Bracht Black (then Stephens), 1988-89 Chamber President, passed the gavel to Clay Gillis. *Gillis was later killed in a private plane accident at Hobby Airport in Houston.*
- MP wrote a column about his grandmother's visit and her trip with him on a fire call.

## JULY

- MP, the outgoing Rotary president, was named Rotarian of the Year.
- The TMM opened to a full house. The main building was named the Sorenson Building in honor of James H. Sorenson, TMM's chairman of the board.
- New banners attached to light standards gave downtown Rockport a new look.

# 30 YEARS THROUGH THE NEWS/LENS

Bill Christian, Susie Bracht Black (then Stephens), and James H. Sorenson Jr. were all smiles the day the TMM opened.

- Seaweed had to be hand-raked from the Rockport Beach Park. The City of Rockport purchased a new beach rake a few weeks later.
- The Rockport Lions Club July 4th Barbecue at Veterans Park was well attended.
- A new playground complex was under construction at the Rockport Beach Park.
- A car and its driver plunged into the harbor, the first of five accidents in a 77-hour period.
- The production by the Tri-County Narcotics Task Force was ranked fifth in the state, behind only Dallas, Fort Worth, Houston and San Antonio.
- Lunch prices at RFJHS were raised from $1 to $1.25.
- Reverend and Mrs. Richard Giller arrived to pastor Fulton Community Church.
- The Economic Development Corporation proposed construction of a multi-use facility.
- Area shrimpers formed a blockade in protest of TEDs.
- The mural on the north wall of Treasure Islander was completed. *This building is the former Roaten Drug Store.*

- A man featured on *America's Most Wanted* television show was arrested after the owners of a shrimp boat in Fulton Harbor recognized him as the new deck hand.

## AUGUST

- First National Bank was robbed. Charles LaBounty, Vice-President, was held hostage by James Dale Pridgen, 46, of Rockport. Pridgen demanded $30,000 for LaBounty's release. Pridgen was captured in Nuevo Laredo, shortly after releasing LaBounty.

James Dale Pridgen, the suspect in the First National Bank robbery, was caught and returned to the AC jail.

- Walmart, located on Business SH 35 at Traylor Boulevard, was remodeled. *That store is now vacant.*
- The Hoopes-Smith House received its historical designation.
- A new law, which restricted children from riding in the bed of a pickup, was approved after an accident occurred in front of Cinema 35.
- Almost 8,000 bags of concrete were placed along the shoreline of the ANWR to limit erosion.

# 30 YEARS THROUGH THE NEWS/LENS

- The Fulton-Bruhl House received a historical marker.
- A Houston man was killed in a fiery crash when he struck an 18-wheeler on SH 35 near the Swiss Chocolate Villa. *Companion Animal Clinic is now located in that building.*
- Buster Gillis was selected ACND chairman.
- The Town of Fulton approved its plan to adopt 911 Service.
- Charles Steward joined the staff of RP. *He later left RP and returned in 2011. He died of a heart attack on July 29, 2013.*
- A Navy pilot made an emergency landing at the AC airport.
- A FVFD truck was stolen, and then recovered. Terry Oates was apprehended.
- Carolyn Behee retired from the RFCC after 10 years of service.

**SEPTEMBER**

- The inaugural *HummerBird Celebration* drew a large crowd.
- The north entrance to Cove Harbor neared completion.
- RP selected student reporters to write monthly columns about news occurring on their school campuses.
- A community cleanup program was discussed.

Sam Walton, Walmart founder, paid a visit to his Rockport store. That building is now vacant.

# 1989: YEAR SIX

- Capt. Ted Appel and Capt. John Howell were upset with the ACND for allowing Deep Sea Headquarters to lease a boat slip to run charters for visitors to see the Whooping Cranes.
- The Economic Development Corporation held a public hearing to receive input about three projects—a multi-purpose facility, a public golf course, and a community foundation.

## OCTOBER

- Ceil Frost donated $200,000 in support of the proposed local YMCA.
- RCC donated a golf cart to the ACISD to use as a Pirate Ship.
- Sam Walton, Walmart founder, visited his Rockport store.
- Larry Sinclair, an undercover officer, was assigned to the RFHS campus. *Sinclair is now a Lieutenant with the RPD.*
- First National Bank's historical marker was unveiled on the Bank's 100th Birthday.
- The Rockport City Council reviewed the City's first Five-year Wastewater Capital Improvement Plan.
- (Brothers) Fred and James Bracht, retired from Bracht Lumber Company.

## NOVEMBER

- *The Pelican* tour boat opened for business.
- Aransas County Medical Services, Inc. (ACMSI), or *The Little Old Ladies in Tennis Shoes*, prepared for the annual ACEMS Bazaar.

## DECEMBER

- The lighting of the 75-foot-tall Children's Christmas Tree was the focal point of the inaugural *Celebration of Lights*.

# 30 YEARS THROUGH THE NEWS/LENS

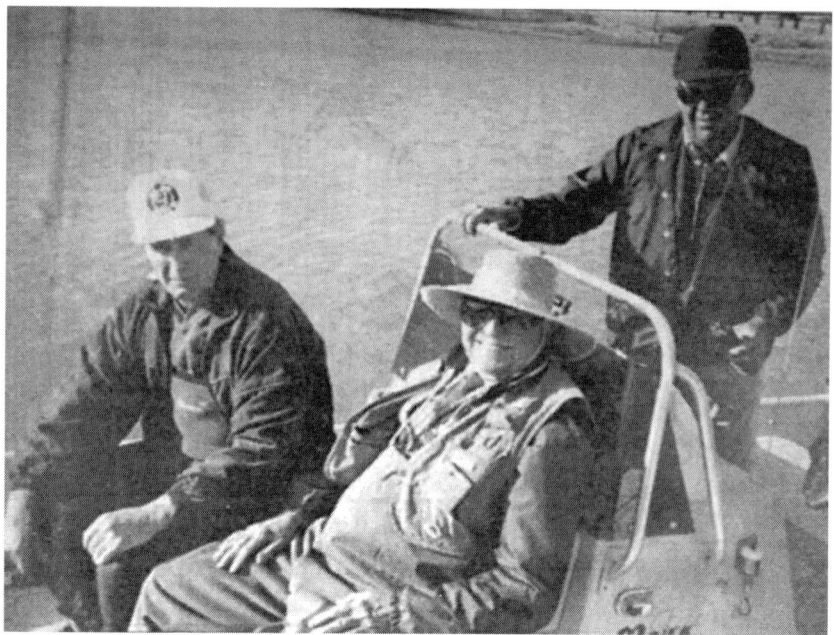

President George H.W. Bush and Perry R. Bass caught their redfish limits in local bays.

- ❏ TxDOT proposed widening FM 881.
- ❏ President George H.W. Bush caught his limit of redfish while fishing in local bays.

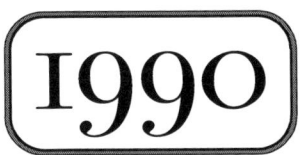

## JANUARY

- More than 14,000 visitors toured the TMM during its first six months of operation.
- ACISD Trustees discussed the possible construction of a wellness center and pool on land across from the bus barn.
- A theft ring was busted, which cleared 40 burglaries.
- Halo-Flight announced it was in danger of closing.
- The RVFD responded to a grease fire at Rockport Elementary.
- Virginia Shivers, the only female to serve as AC Sheriff, was treated to a retirement party after 16 years of service at First National Bank.
- S&W Disposal's services were described as "unacceptable."
- Plans to develop a Juvenile Detox Center were discussed.
- Rex Littleton, Rockport Public Works Director, retired.
- Golden Needles Quilting Shop opened.

## FEBRUARY

- RFHS dropped from 4A to 3A.
- John Witte was sworn in as AC's new road administrator.
- Protests were heard when a company proposed drilling in California Hole, a popular fishing spot.
- Rob Robison, Rockport's City Manager, applied for the city manager's position in Ingleside.
- Leggett Light Channel dredging was halted due to issues with the Corps of Engineers' Permit.

# 30 YEARS THROUGH THE NEWS/LENS

- James Samsel, Rockport resident, was charged with real estate fraud in Arizona.
- RCA organizers planned for the inaugural *Tour of Homes*.
- The AC Airport acquired a VOR/TAC Navigation System.

**MARCH**

- TxDOT approved the FM 881 Widening Project.
- The City of Rockport Tax Rollback Election passed with 27 percent of registered voters casting votes.
- Debbie Littleton was named Rockport City Secretary.
- The Candlestick Park subdivision was developed.
- The *Third Coast Racing Club Oval Championships* was held at the Rockport Beach Park.
- Helen Braffett, retiring Rockport City Secretary, was honored at a luncheon.

**APRIL**

- Officials from the planned Formosa Plant in Calhoun County held a hearing about possible environmental threats to AC.
- MP wrote a column supporting the construction of a new high school as the best long-term decision for educating our youth.
- A woman was killed on FM 1069 when a tilt-flat trailer came loose from a truck and struck her vehicle.
- AC Commissioners heard demands for a leash law.
- Buster Gillis defeated Danny Adams in the GOP Primary election for AC Judge.
- An infant found buried near Palm Harbor appeared to have been beaten.
- John Mitchell was honored for 50 years of Perfect Attendance in the Rotary Club.

## 1990: YEAR SEVEN

- Annette Hegen, seafood specialist with the TPWD, met Julia Childs in Atlanta.
- Matt Aycock, RFHS golfer, signed a letter of intent to play golf for the University of Texas.
- Crime Stoppers of AC held its kickoff event. MP was the organization's first president.
- The TPWD asked the ACND for help in paving the parking area adjacent to its lab at Rockport Harbor.

**MAY**

- George Martin defeated L.E. Casterline 659 to 408 votes in the Rockport mayoral election.
- Crime Stoppers of AC began printing its *Crime of the Week* in the RP.
- Bobby Flanagan, longtime RFHS coach and athletic director, retired.
- The RFHS choir was rated *Best in the Nation*.
- Robbie Hattenbach signed to play football at Hardin-Simmons University.
- The City of Rockport studied the possible annexation of Key Allegro.
- A boy saved the life of a baby, who fell into Rockport Harbor.
- Clayton Williams, gubernatorial candidate, made a brief stop at the AC Airport.
- Wes Williams, Rockport Patrolman, was suspended following a shooting at a Circle K Convenience Store.

**JUNE**

- Bracht Lumber held a grand re-opening.
- George Martin, newly-elected Rockport Mayor, called for a community cleanup.

# 30 YEARS THROUGH THE NEWS/LENS

- The FVFD had the fastest pumper racing team in the state.
- Raymond Jaramillo, TPWD Game Warden, rescued Chelcie Newton, a Rockport 4H Club member, after a tubing accident in a river.

Susie Bracht Black (then Stephens) and Bryan Bracht purchased Bracht Lumber from family members.

- The Wendells were honored as benefactors of their fireworks show for 25 years.
- *Clean Sweep* netted 10 tons of trash.
- The Rockport Jaycees repaired the band shell at Rockport Beach Park.
- A potential buyer of RYSCO decided against purchasing the company.

**JULY**

- The 750-plus sleeping rooms in Rockport-Fulton were filled to capacity during the Fourth of July weekend. *Today approximately 1,500 sleeping rooms are available in Rockport-Fulton.*

## 1990: YEAR SEVEN

Rockport Jaycees repaired the band shell as a club project.

- The *21st Rockport Art Festival* endured volatile weather.
- The Rockport Lion's Club BBQ Pit at Veteran's Park was in need of repair. The community's help was sought.
- U.S. Senator Lloyd Bentsen visited AC.
- Dr. Fred Warren was honored for his service with a *Special Day*.
- Cosme Cavazos of Corpus Christi caught a large tarpon in Copano Bay.
- T.J. Johnson was injured in a travel trailer fire.
- A crowd gathered when a rare bird, a blue-footed booby, was spotted at Rockport Harbor.
- Eighteen ultra-light aircraft visited the AC Airport.
- Peggy Manning won $10,000 in the *85th Anniversary Texas Millionaire Contest*.
- Bob Lynch resigned his post as RFCC Executive Director.
- The ANWR was expanded by 3,764 acres with the purchase of Rancho LaBahia.
- Valley Transit Company and National Bus Lines began daily service to other cities from Ray's Texaco in downtown Rockport. *CJ's Sign and Crane Service is now located in that building. The bus now stops at the Stripes store on Market Street.*

# 30 YEARS THROUGH THE NEWS/LENS

## AUGUST

- Rip Harrison, local artist, passed away.
- A local Crime Stoppers tip led to an arrest for selling heroin from a hotel.
- Cosme Cavazos caught another tarpon in Copano Bay.
- The Connie Hagar Historical Marker was dedicated at Little Bay.
- The death of a couple near the Big Tree was ruled a murder/suicide.
- The Rockport-Fulton Evening Lions Club received its charter.
- Ruth Davis bought Scotty's Lock & Key.
- MP wrote a column about his daughter's first day at ABC School.

Cosme Cavazos caught two large tarpon in Copano Bay within 30 days.

## SEPTEMBER

- Corky's Restaurant in downtown Rockport closed its doors when Corky retired.
- Diane Probst was hired as RFCC's Executive Director.
- Jan Wendell placed 118th out of 600 at the World Bridge Championship.
- John D. Wendell, AC Judge, who served in that position for almost 40 years, was honored on *John Wendell Day* with a reception at the AC Courthouse.

## 1990: YEAR SEVEN

The historical marker for Connie Hagar, "The Bird Lady," was unveiled next to Little Bay.

- Rockport Coast Guard Auxiliary Flotilla 79 was named *Best in the Nation*.
- Jesus Moroles, local granite sculptor, was commissioned to create the Houston Police Officers' Memorial.

### OCTOBER

- A fire in a Fulton home killed a grandmother and two children.
- Ann Robbins was named bank manager at the First Interstate Bank.

### NOVEMBER

- The Neon Teen Club opened in the Harbor Oaks Village Shopping Center.
- Liza Pina won first place and set a new record in Cross Country Running at the District Track Meet.
- AC Commissioners agreed to split the cost of a new fuel depot with the City of Rockport.

# 30 YEARS THROUGH THE NEWS/LENS

- Oscar Trevino, an RFHS teacher and coach, was arrested for indecency with a child.
- The Rockport GI Forum installed air conditioning.
- Agnes A. "Tony" Harden, Democrat, was elected AC Judge. "Tony" served as District Clerk before becoming a judge.
- The AC Municipal Utilities District filed for bankruptcy.
- The *La Tortuga*, Scow Sloop, was launched and christened by the TMM.
- The ACISD established a Saturday School Program.
- The *Wharf Cat* began offering Whooping Crane Trips from Rockport Harbor.
- The renovated band shell at the Rockport Beach Park was dedicated. Tommy Shults, the original designer, spoke at the dedication.
- Bernie DeForrest, ACND Harbormaster, retired.

*La Tortuga*, Scow Sloop, was launched in the ski basin and then christened by TMM officials.

- Three shrimp boats were sunk at Cove Harbor due to a tug accident.

**DECEMBER**

- British writers visited AC to view nature.
- Rusty Hamilton resigned as RFHS athletic director and head football coach.

# 30 YEARS THROUGH THE NEWS/LENS

## JANUARY

- RFHS and RFJHS students held a *Walk Out for Peace* in opposition to war. The students were treated as truants.
- Rob Robison, Rockport City Manager, was called to active duty with the U.S. Marines. Department heads led the City in his absence.
- The body of a 55-year-old man was found at Fulton Harbor. His 37-year-old wife was found in the harbor days later.
- Sales tax rebate checks in January were $27,480.68 for AC, $37,122.88 for Rockport, and $3,144.61 for Fulton. *In January 2014, AC received $191,029.86, Rockport received $159,037.46, and Fulton received $14,627.20.*
- The Sea Gun property was for sale for $350,000. The five-acre property included the marina, restaurant, meeting hall and buildings.
- Rick McLester was honored for his 18 years of service as RVFD Chief.

## FEBRUARY

- The Master Gardener Program began operations in AC.
- AC Commissioners approved a 35-foot wide entrance to Memorial Park.
- Rockport Bank was closed, purchased, and reopened as the Bank of Corpus Christi.
- Bidding for the construction of the SH 35 bypass was announced as beginning in the fall.

# 1991: YEAR EIGHT

- Bob Pyssen was hired as RFHS athletic director and head football coach.
- Tim Jayroe, RPD Chief, was named Acting City Manager in the absence of Rob Robison.
- Animal Control Officers warned of a distemper threat.
- Parents spoke out regarding the ACISD's proposed Early Childhood Center format.
- Due to low demand, Coastal Bend Hospital closed the local Urgent Care Center.

## MARCH
- LSD, being sold at RFHS, was seized.
- It was reported animal cruelty was widespread in AC.
- Local leaders were "cool" regarding a proposal to build a public golf course.
- The Rockport City Council discussed creating a Countywide Park System.
- Concern was raised regarding rabies in the area.

## APRIL
- Cathy Lowe was named new administrator at the TMM.
- A year-round concessionaire at the Rockport Beach Park was approved.

RP received its historical marker in 1991.

# 30 YEARS THROUGH THE NEWS/LENS

## MAY

- RP's Historical Marker was unveiled.
- The City of Rockport approved its HOT Contract with the RFCC. The Town of Fulton terminated its contract with the RFCC.
- The AC Appraisal District explained the reasons for the high property appraisals.
- Rob Robison, Rockport City Manager, returned from the Iraq war and back to his job.
- MP wrote a column under the headline "Who's Responsible in this Ridiculous Healthcare Situation?"
- The Saltwater Pavilion was ready for use. Rent was $150 on weekends, and $100 during the week. *The rent is now $600 on weekends and $400 Mondays-Thursdays.*
- Dave Segler and Charles Roe retired after serving many years with the ACISD.
- Oak Crest Nursing Center opened.

## JUNE

- Jackson Seafood sold its Gulf Shrimp Boats, marking the end of an era.

The inaugural Rockport-Fulton Air Show was another unique event during the Fourth of July weekend.

## 1991: YEAR EIGHT

- A new air show in the skies over Rockport Beach Park was planned for July 4.
- The Rockport-Fulton Good Samaritan Center opened for business.

### JULY

- Henry Cisneros, former San Antonio Mayor, was the keynote speaker at the RFCC's Annual Banquet.

U-Haul trailers promoted the HummerBird Celebration. Some of the trailers are still on the road today.

- Rockport was ranked 20th in the state for the number of long-term visitors.
- U-Haul announced the promotion of the HummerBird Celebration on select trailers. The mobile billboards have a 15-plus year lifespan, and can still be seen on the road today.
- Fred Hartman, RP Owner, died July 31, 1991.
- AC Commissioners proposed using the available half-cent sales tax for indigent healthcare.
- Bob Hewes, AC Sheriff, was named *Sheriff of the Year.*

# 30 YEARS THROUGH THE NEWS/LENS

- TxDOT moved its operations in AC to a new facility on FM 3036.

## AUGUST

- More than 6,000 people jammed into Rockport Beach Park to watch the Memorial Drag Boat Races.
- Redistricting forced changes. AC's 17,892 population was separated into four precincts of approximately 4,473 residents.
- The election imposing a half cent sales tax to help fund AC's indigent healthcare passed with a 755 to 713 vote.
- The local unemployment rate was 3.5 percent.
- A new state law went into effect requiring proof of liability insurance in all vehicles.

## SEPTEMBER

- MP wrote a column about the passing of his Oma (grandmother).

The Historical Mile March included the dedication of historical markers at five churches.

## 1991: YEAR EIGHT

- Rockport Sea & Spray opened.
- The AC Courthouse Annex opened.
- Bob Hewes, AC Sheriff, announced his retirement.
- Emery Real Estate opened.
- During budget discussions about salary increases, Agnes A. "Tony" Harden, AC Judge, became very vocal, while facing an angry crowd.
- The *Historical Mile March* included the dedication of historical markers for five churches.

## OCTOBER

- An estranged husband killed a mother of three children.
- The Boy Scout Hut was vandalized.
- AC Commissioners approved reducing the number of Justices of the Peace from four to two.
- A fire destroyed a residence in Palm Harbor.
- AC Commissioners approved charging a HOT on hotels in the county.
- George Martin, Rockport Mayor, visited Rockport's Australian Sister City, Beachport.
- The Fennessey Ranch began developing a wildlife preserve.
- The Town of Fulton annexed an area bordered by the south side of Broadway Street, the south side of Palmetto Street, Highway 35, and Aransas Bay.

## NOVEMBER

- Ten inches of rain flooded roads and toppled trees.
- Students graduated from ACISD's first daytime GED Class.
- The Resolution Trust Corp. auctioned the Oak Bay Condos.

# 30 YEARS THROUGH THE NEWS/LENS

- Rob Robison, Rockport City Manager, resigned his position for a job in New Jersey.
- The Fulton Town Council approved its HOT contract with the RFCC.
- Tommy Aycock, RCC golf pro, announced he would play on the Senior PGA Tour.

Winter visitors always look forward to the Town of Fulton's annual Winter Texan Fish Fry.

## DECEMBER

- ANWR personnel reported the arrival of 133 Whooping Cranes.
- K-PLAY announced it would be off the air for six months. *The station later closed and no other radio station has located in AC.*
- The new 911 System was tested.
- In a sting operation, seven businesses were nailed for selling alcohol to minors.

## 1991: YEAR EIGHT

- AC Commissioners approved a HOT rate of six percent.
- The Rockport City Council appointed Walter Hill as Interim City Manager.
- Heldenfels Brothers was awarded the bid for a 4,500-foot taxiway at the AC Airport.
- Enron announced funding for an Environmental Education & Research Center at Matagorda.
- Mary and Monte Taylor presented a cookbook produced during the Exxon Valdez Oil Spill in Alaska.
- AC Airport personnel and Road and Bridge workers were laid off.

# 30 YEARS THROUGH THE NEWS/LENS

## JANUARY

- Following a presentation by the Aransas Pass City Manager, AC Commissioners approved a resolution for a prison near Aransas Pass.
- TxDOT announced construction on the SH 35 bypass could begin as early as March.
- Owners of the Hoopes-Smith home announced it would become a bed and breakfast.
- A Rockport City Charter Election was held and all proposed changes were approved.
- The YMCA presence in AC was growing. More than 200 youth registered to play in the YMCA Basketball League.
- Harold Picton was sworn in as AC Commissioner replacing the retiring Pete Sanders.
- The Lions Club BBQ pit was moved to Memorial Park.
- Flooding in AC caused thousands of dollars damage to roads.
- RP increased its newsstand price to 50 cents.
- Father Hanh Van Pham was ordained into the priesthood.

## FEBRUARY

- Emergency 911 Service was activated on February 5.
- Due to large amounts of rain, overflowing septic systems showed the glaring need for County-wide Sanitary Sewers.
- AC Commissioners appointed a committee to develop a County Drainage Plan.

## 1992: YEAR NINE

9-1-1 decals were placed on patrol cars once the emergency number was operational in AC.

- A group of interested residents attended a presentation about the establishment of a YMCA in Rockport-Fulton.
- The Rockport City Council learned repairs to streets damaged by high water could cost more than $100,000.
- The open Rockport City Manager position drew 35 applications.
- The RFHS Pirate basketball team won the District Championship.
- Local juveniles faced stiff punishment for prank calls.
- James Koonce, Live Oak Elementary Principal, was honored for 20 years of service.
- SPARTS, the transit system, began service.
- A letter written during the Civil War was donated to the AC Historical Commission.
- A Committee was formed to investigate providing sewer service to *No Man's Land. That area between the city limits of Rockport and Fulton has since been annexed by the City of Rockport.*

# 30 YEARS THROUGH THE NEWS/LENS

The Rockport-Fulton YMCA received its charter during a ceremony in Corpus Christi.

## MARCH

- M.H. Pete Gildon was selected as Rockport's City Manager.
- The RFCC celebrated its 40th Anniversary.
- The City of Rockport/AC Compost Site was opened.
- The RFHS tennis team advanced to the UIL State Tournament.
- AC was designated a disaster area due to the recent flooding.
- Dr. Steve Smith was selected as the first YMCA Chairman.
- The Rockport-Fulton YMCA found a new home in the old Shapemakers Building on Market Street next to Rockport City Hall.
- The Rockport-Fulton YMCA received its Charter.

## APRIL

- Father Deane was transferred to St. Joseph's Catholic Church in Port Aransas.

## 1992: YEAR NINE

The Easter Sunrise Service on Rockport Beach is a well-attended event.

- After 20 minutes, law enforcement officers arrested an inmate escapee.
- Submerged vehicles were recovered from a local pond.

**MAY**

- Local governments received more than $220,000 in FEMA funds due to flood damages.
- The Rockport-Fulton YMCA held its grand opening.
- RFHS students spoke out against teachers smoking. They also wanted long shorts to be included in the dress code.
- The Rockport City Council heard about health concerns due to animals being allowed on the beach.
- State Rep. Todd Hunter announced a push for tougher DWI Laws.
- Gary Mysorski was named Rockport-Fulton YMCA Director.
- The Environmental Protection Agency sought a delay in the construction of the Highway 35 bypass.

# 30 YEARS THROUGH THE NEWS/LENS

A rain event dumped way too much water in too short a time period. Runoff destroyed a part of this home on Fulton Beach Road.

- The Marguerite Sours Foundation's first grant was awarded to ABC Learning Center.
- The State of Texas began selling lottery tickets.
- Heavy rains destroyed part of a home on Fulton Beach Road. The rain also caused havoc in Fulton.
- First National Bank merged with Victoria Bankshares.
- Two AC residents were killed in a collision on SH 35 near Cove Harbor. *That portion of the highway was designated Business SH 35 once the SH 35 bypass was opened.*
- The ACISD began allowing students to wear long shorts year-round.
- The RFHS band traveled to Orlando and won high honors.

**JUNE**
- A Trash-a-Thon raised $1,865 and netted 193 bags of trash.

- The HummerBird Celebration logo was added to 200 more U-Haul trailers.
- Property for a shelter was donated anonymously to the Humane Society of Aransas County.
- A traffic stop resulted in the detention of 23 undocumented workers. They were being transported in the back of a small, windowless U-Haul truck.
- The necessary permits were granted for Phase 1 of the SH 35 bypass as a relief route.

**JULY**
- Africanized honeybees were identified in AC.
- ACISD trustees approved purchasing the Oaks Office Park.
- Area code changes were announced.
- AC severed the county's ties with the San Patricio Community Action Agency.
- RP won the *Keep Texas Beautiful Award* in the Media Division.
- The RFCC announced plans for 12 annual events at the Rockport Beach Park.
- The Rockport City Council hired a contractor to shred hills of brush into compost.
- Attempts to declare AC a disaster area following heavy rains were rejected.
- Stanley Stores Inc. purchased the Harbor Oaks Village Shopping Center.

**AUGUST**
- A pilot recycling test program was announced, which included 150 residents.
- Approximately 4,000 people watched the Drag Boat Races at the Rockport Beach Park.

# 30 YEARS THROUGH THE NEWS/LENS

- Curbside mail delivery in the RCC was approved.
- The Town of Fulton and the FVFD were at odds regarding the ownership and operation of the Paws and Taws Building.
- A marijuana greenhouse was found on Glass Avenue.
- One person was killed in a bizarre car crash on the Copano Causeway Fishing Pier.
- The AC Clean Team received a grant to make improvements to Veterans Park.
- A local delegation traveled to Austin to speak in support of continued funding for the Fulton Mansion.
- Pacific Southwest Bank acquired First Interstate Bank. *Pacific Southwest Bank is now Prosperity Bank.*
- The State Park Fund awarded $159,395 for improvements to Tiger Field.

**SEPTEMBER**

- R.C. Deal, developer, announced plans to build a retirement community near Lamar.
- Bahia Bay homeowners demanded repairs be made to the roads in their subdivision.
- The City of Rockport's proposed sign ordinance caused controversy.

**OCTOBER**

- The TPWD shot a video at the Fulton Mansion.
- The Peggy Bloch Memorial was dedicated at the TMM.
- Four women were robbed on the fifth tee box at RCC.
- AC Commissioners endorsed FM 881 becoming a state highway.
- Bob Hewes, retiring AC Sheriff, served as the Grand Marshall of the Seafair Parade.

## 1992: YEAR NINE

Bob Hewes, retiring AC Sheriff, was Grand Marshal of the Seafair Parade.

- Analisa Kennedy was the first woman to be named *Sportsman of the Year* at the local Ducks Unlimited Banquet.
- The Rockport Art Center changed its name to RCA.

**NOVEMBER**

- Officials of Corpus Christi State University, an upper level university, announced it would become a four-year college in 1994. *The college then became part of the Texas A&M System and renamed Texas A&M University–Corpus Christi.*
- David Petrusaitis was elected AC Sheriff.
- Site plans for the Rockport-Fulton YMCA were approved.
- R.C. Deal revived the Goose Island condominiums.
- The RFHS Pirate football team won the District Championship for the first time in 20 years.
- The City of Rockport approved an ordinance for flashing lights to be installed in school zones.
- A bomb threat was received at RFJHS.

# 30 YEARS THROUGH THE NEWS/LENS

- ACISD Trustees approved requesting bids to renovate the Oaks Office Park to be used as a new school campus. *Pre-K through Kindergarten children are housed on that campus, now called Little Bay Primary School.*
- Construction of the Fulton Harbor Boat Ramp was completed.
- Margaret (Seward) (Terry) Skeete, Rockport native, was named *Oldest Living American. Born in 1878, she was 115 years, 192 days old when she died in 1994.*

**DECEMBER**

- First National Bank officially merged with Victoria Bank & Trust, a historic bank alliance.
- A man was found dead on a boat near San Jose Island.
- Recently-annexed Fulton residents voiced their concerns about sanitary sewer service.
- The Holly Day Festival in downtown Rockport drew a large crowd.
- RP requested entries for a *Special Christmas Story* contest. Pat Nuffer's story was selected.
- *ABC World News Tonight* visited John Howell, Captain of the *Pisces*.
- FM 881 was officially designated a state highway.

# 1993

## JANUARY

- The Attorney General of Texas gave an opinion stating the ACND was not allowed to use tax revenues to pay bulk heading expenses at Cove Harbor.
- Two people were killed in an accident on New Year's Eve at the intersection of FM 136 and FM 188.
- The Rockport Sailing Club changed its name to Rockport Yacht Club.
- Two people were injured in a PHI helicopter incident at the AC Airport.
- Dan McGee, ACND Commissioner, attacked the $1 Leases awarded to nonprofit organizations such as the RCA, TMM, RFCC, and the Woman's Club.
- The Texas Outdoor Writers Association Convention was held in Rockport and Fulton with more than 125 outdoor writers attending.
- Sears stopped catalog sales.
- Mandi Mills was nominated to West Point.
- Interest was high for the formation of a new birders club.
- Real estate sales hit a record high of $24.2 million.

## FEBRUARY

- A new Kiwanis Club was chartered.
- The AC Youth Support Center combined efforts with the Rockport-Fulton YMCA.

# 30 YEARS THROUGH THE NEWS/LENS

- Louis Frederick Kihneman III, Sacred Heart Catholic Church priest, was elevated to Monsignor.
- The Rockport-Fulton Good Samaritans moved into its new building on Ann Street.
- A tree was planted at Veterans Park in honor of Max Kluge, Sr.
- Daniel Vasquez, RFHS running back, signed a letter of intent to play football at Texas A&I University.
- The *For the Love of Quilts Show* was held at the Saltwater Pavilion.
- AC Commissioners approved placing a fire station in the Palm Harbor area.
- Gary Cooper presented a plan to revive the Economic Development Corporation. The plan was rejected.
- New signs, upgraded with flashers, were installed at the intersection of FM 881 and FM 136.
- Stacey Johnson's singing talent led her to Nashville.
- Leroy Hillyer rescued Martin Solis from a fire.

## MARCH

- Controversy between the Town of Fulton and the FVFD regarding funding for the Paws and Taws Building continued. Gary Cooper said Fulton should stop spending Fulton's HOT money to operate Paws and Taws.
- Chad Stutzman signed a letter of intent to play football at Angelo State.
- ACISD Trustees considered hiring a truant officer.
- During a storm, lightning struck nine homes in AC.
- The Coastal Classic Car Show was held at the Rockport Beach Park

## 1993: YEAR TEN

- The Rockport City Council approved a new smoking ordinance.
- Companion Animal Clinic moved into the former Swiss Chocolate Villa building. *It remains at the same location.*
- AC Commissioners approved restrictions on sex shops.
- ACND Commissioners stuck to their guns regarding the proposed charges to the TPWD for its lease at Rockport Harbor.
- The City of Rockport and Town of Fulton received Proud Community Awards from *Keep Texas Beautiful*.

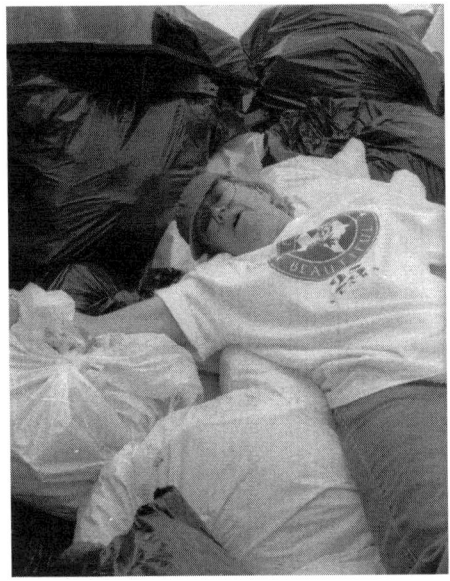

Cleaning up trash in AC was the focus of the AC Clean Team. Its members' work led to numerous statewide awards.

The popular Big Fisherman Restaurant was destroyed by fire. It was rebuilt, but is now closed.

# 30 YEARS THROUGH THE NEWS/LENS

## APRIL

- A massive blaze destroyed the Big Fisherman Restaurant on April 14, killing numerous exotic animals.
- ACISD Trustees named R-F Intermediate School as the new campus housing fifth and sixth grade students. This school was previously the Oaks Office Park. *Fourth and fifth graders now attend Fulton Learning Center and sixth graders attend RFMS.*
- Gary Cooper proposed forming a *Community Economic Development Corporation* after his ideas for reviving the Economic Development Corporation were rejected.
- The RFCC sought nominees for new awards—*Citizen of the Year* and *Chamber Member of the Year*—to be given at the RFCC's Annual Banquet.
- A man jumped off the Copano Causeway to retrieve two surfboards, which blew off his car while crossing the bridge. He caught up with his surfboards, but the tide carried him toward Bayside. He was rescued unharmed.
- The Fulton Town Council approved distributing HOT funds to the FVFD to operate the Paws and Taws building.
- The City of Rockport adopted the newly commissioned *USS Warrior* and provided family activities for sailors.

## MAY

- An Ice Box convenience store was robbed by an armed thief.
- The kitchen area at the Mid-Beach Pavilion was saved when a passerby noticed smoke coming from the building.
- AC was battered twice by rain as well as 60 mph winds.
- The RFHS One-Act Play placed second in the State UIL Contest.

## 1993: YEAR TEN

- The owners of the Big Fisherman Restaurant were upset with the Animal Order approved by AC Commissioners in the wake of the fire at the restaurant.
- 1993 was called the best year for fishing along the coast since the 1960s.
- The State of Texas named Gene Johnson *Airport Manager of the Year.*
- Mandi Mills was named *Sportsman of the Year* at the RFHS All-Sports Banquet.
- Brett Phillips, RFHS pitching ace, led the Pirates to the Area Playoffs.
- Sam Spears signed with Concordia Lutheran College to play basketball.
- RFHS graduated 116 students.

### JUNE

- The Rockport-Fulton YMCA celebrated its first anniversary.
- The ACND learned the beach was eroding at 9.42 feet per year.
- TxDOT and the Friends of Connie Hagar planted native plants at a roadside park on Business SH 35.
- Father Nguyen, Vietnamese Catholic priest, passed away.
- Larry's Sharpening & Repair opened.
- Ceil Frost was named *Citizen of the Year* at the RFCC's Annual Banquet.
- Tropical Storm Arlene soaked AC.
- Headstart Daycare opened.

### JULY

- A County-wide Road Maintenance Program was studied.

# 30 YEARS THROUGH THE NEWS/LENS

- Forever Green Landscaping and RP won the top *Keep Texas Beautiful Awards* in their category.
- RP introduced its new *Extra* edition, which included its classified section. It was distributed in Aransas Pass and Ingleside.
- Coldwell Banker Island Realtors opened.
- New signage designated FM 881 as a dual route with FM 1069 from Business SH 35 to Ingleside.
- Friends of Connie Hagar purchased the property formerly owned by the late Connie Hagar.
- Property owners in *No Man's Land* sought annexation from the City of Rockport.
- The RFCC hosted a *Comedy Night* at the Paws and Taws to raise funds for new Welcome signs.

## AUGUST

- Castaways announced plans to construct a new building on its property.
- The ACND approved transferring the Paws and Taws lease from the FVFD to the RFCC.
- AC Commissioners approved the RFCC's purchase of Paws and Taws.
- The Redfish Bay Chapter of the GCCA held its first banquet at the Paws and Taws.
- A Demonstration Garden located at the roadside park on Business SH 35 officially opened.
- The search for two AC Jail escapees continued.

## SEPTEMBER

- The AC Jail was cited for numerous violations, most of which were corrected.

# 1993: YEAR TEN

- Les "Googles" Cole, Fulton Mayor, resigned his office to make it possible for Katherine McLester to become the first female mayor of Fulton.
- Third Coast Real Estate opened.
- ACSO deputies made a record-setting bust, confiscating 213 pounds of marijuana.

The former Oaks Office Park was converted into an ACISD campus, opening first as Rockport-Fulton Intermediate School.

- RP's Lynda Frome passed away after losing her battle with cancer.

## OCTOBER

- Free recycling began at the AC Transfer Station.
- Discussions were held by AC Commissioners about a bi-county jail with Refugio County.
- The new Rockport-Fulton Intermediate School was dedicated. *That campus is now Little Bay Primary.*
- Shania Twain performed at Seafair.
- Anthony's By The Sea Bed and Breakfast opened.

# 30 YEARS THROUGH THE NEWS/LENS

- The Fulton Community Church celebrated its 50th Anniversary.
- A fire at the Caspary-Wendell, Inc. building at Cove Harbor caused heavy damage.
- Bracht Lumber Company was burglarized during the Halloween Weekend.

**NOVEMBER**

- Curbside recycling began in Rockport.
- Grace Vivian Picton, lifelong Rockport resident, celebrated her 100th birthday.
- Raulie Irwin was hired to contribute historical selections in the RP.

**DECEMBER**

- Les "Googles" Cole, Fulton Mayor, decided to stay in his elected position as mayor.
- A groundbreaking was held at the site of the proposed south fire station on Freeze Lane.
- Val Jean Eaton, AC Clerk, retired after a 32-year career.
- AC vehicles were burned at the county barn.
- The RVFD purchased new uniforms.
- The front page of the December 25 edition of RP was printed in green and red ink.

# 1994

The opening of the expanded Castaways was a big event, but nothing like the opening of the organization's new building on Market Street in 2014.

## JANUARY

- The ACSO warned residents about unexploded mortar shells found in the AC.
- Cory Cruser, RFHS choir member, was the first freshman in RFHS history named to the UIL All-State Choir.
- The RFCC Charmers, a group of volunteer Visitor Center greeters, were formed.
- Castaways opened at its new location with a *Bless this House Ceremony*.
- Moore Than Feed opened.

# 30 YEARS THROUGH THE NEWS/LENS

- Pam Heard was named RCA Executive Director.
- The City of Rockport helped the Friends of Connie Hagar with the purchase of the site of Hagar's former residence on Church Street.
- Dat Nguyen, RFHS football star, signed a letter of intent to play football at Texas A&M University.
- The RCA reopened after being remodeled.
- The San Patricio County Juvenile Center opened.

**FEBRUARY**

- Ellen Murry was named TMM Director.
- The North American Free Trade Agreement was discussed at a RFCC meeting.
- ACISD Trustees presented three facility options ranging from $22 to $24 million.
- A deer was spooked and ran through a window at Coldwell Banker Island Real Estate.
- The Fulton Town Council agreed to buy the Paws and Taws building.
- The inaugural *Rockport-Fulton Festival of the Cranes and Other Shorebirds* was held. *This event is now held in Port Aransas.*
- A historical marker was dedicated at the Railroad Depot on Magnolia Street.
- Newspaper curbside recycling began.
- RPD reported 22 cases of criminal mischief in four subdivisions.

**MARCH**

- A new outdoor lifeboat exhibit opened at the TMM.

- A *Downtown Rockport Walking Tour* was announced.

## APRIL

- The City of Rockport investigated implementing one-way traffic off Business SH 35 at the "Y" at SeaAire Shopping Center.
- Maple Street was upgraded to include a sidewalk.
- New gas pumps were installed at the Harbor Oaks Village Shopping Center. *These pumps have since been removed.*
- The Sid Richardson Foundation granted the RCA $100,000.
- The Texas Association of Campground Owners held its Spring Convention at Circle W RV Park.
- ABC Learning Center added a full-day preschool program.
- The Linden Oaks Apartments opened.
- Chris Johnson was named City of Rockport Code Enforcement Officer.
- Asa and Verna Yeamans opened Calm Harbor Real Estate.

## MAY

- The RPD formed a bike patrol for use in and around the Rockport Beach Park.
- The City of Rockport began its Citizens Academy.
- A fire on Key Allegro destroyed three condominium units.
- A San Antonio man, who was asleep in his sleeping bag on the Copano Pier, was accidentally run over by a car driven by the concessionaire.
- The Rockport-Fulton Women's Clinic opened.
- Guy Clark, Nashville songwriter and Rockport native, serenaded the crowd at Music Fest.

# 30 YEARS THROUGH THE NEWS/LENS

**JUNE**

- M.L. "Red" Cashion, NFL Referee, was the keynote speaker at the RFCC Annual Banquet.
- RYSCO, a Rockport landmark, was razed.
- Rockport Cemetery was expanded by two acres.

**JULY**

- The RFHS Choir performed at the Cathedral of Notre Dame in Paris, France.
- A concert by Tim McGraw, a Nashville "up and comer," proposed to be held at the end of Rockport Beach Park, was approved by the Rockport City Council on a 3-2 vote.
- Two women were killed in two separate accidents, 24 hours apart, at the intersection of FM 1069 and SH 188. *RP published an editorial calling for a four-way stop at that intersection. Within two weeks TxDOT installed new four-way stop signs.*
- Rockport's Gospel Force, a quartet made up of RPD members, including Tim Jayroe, Gary Howard, Mark Gilliam, and Larry Sinclair, made its singing debut.
- Dollar General announced one of its stores would open in Harbor Oaks Village Shopping Center.

RYSCO rose above the horizon in downtown Rockport for many years before it was razed.

# 1994: YEAR ELEVEN

- The ACISD bought the former Companion Animal Clinic building.
- Country Club Square donated a portable building for the RFCC's expansion. *That portable building is still in use across the street from the RFCC's current location.*
- Tom Benson, owner of the New Orleans Saints, proposed an 80-acre wildlife refuge at the end of Shell Ridge.
- The AC Clean Team won *Keep Texas Beautiful Awards*.

## AUGUST

- Bank of America–Texas opened. *That bank no longer has a branch located in Rockport-Fulton.*
- A large crowd showed up at Rockport City Hall to protest the City's proposed new sign ordinance.
- Luong's Chinese Restaurant opened in the building, which formerly housed Corky's Restaurant.
- The State funded the *Great Texas Coastal Birding Trail.*

## SEPTEMBER

- ABC News provided national coverage of the HummerBird Celebration.
- The RVFD's new south station opened bearing the name, Raulie L. Irwin.

## OCTOBER

- "Ruby," the school crossing guard since 1978, was recognized.
- Tim McGraw mesmerized a crowd of 3,500 on a Sunday night at Rockport Beach Park. *Tim McGraw has since become a country western music star.*
- A dedication service for the Rockport-Fulton YMCA Property was set. The projected floor plan was presented.

# 30 YEARS THROUGH THE NEWS/LENS

Tim McGraw performed at the Rockport Beach Park before he became an entertainment superstar.

- ❏ A public hearing about the City of Rockport's Plans to annex Moore Farm, Sylvan Heights, or *No Man's Land*, and Aransas Bay Tracts drew a large crowd.
- ❏ A Russian artist won the design contest for new *Welcome* signs.
- ❏ The SH 35 bypass was designated a truck route.

**NOVEMBER**

- ❏ The RFCC's portable building addition was officially opened.
- ❏ Funds were sought to ensure the Big Tree could be fertilized once per year.
- ❏ Maxicorp, Inc. announced plans for a new Bealls store, as well as other tenants at SeaAire Shopping Center.
- ❏ Karen Hall's, ACISD Superintendent, contract was terminated by ACISD Trustees. Norman Spears was named Interim Superintendent.
- ❏ While mowing his yard, Sam Uhl, 70, was attacked by Africanized Killer Bees.

## 1994: YEAR ELEVEN

The SH 35 bypass was officially opened in November 2004.

- The Annual ACMSI Bazaar drew big crowds in support of the ACEMS. *The ACEMS is no longer in service.*
- State officials considered a limited entry plan for bay shrimping.

**DECEMBER**

- MP wrote a column about his first snow skiing experience.
- About 1,000 people attended the Fulton Fish Fry at the Paws and Taws.
- Eunice Hamon, AC Librarian, was honored for her 22 years of service.
- Chano Falcon, ACISD Trustee, asked John Boidy, fellow trustee, to resign.
- The SH 35 bypass Relief Route was officially opened.
- The Town of Fulton cut its HOT contribution to the RFCC from three cents to two cents.
- Drivers charged with DWI would lose their license beginning in 1995.
- Price-Lo Warehouse Foods filed for Chapter 11 Bankruptcy.

# 30 YEARS THROUGH THE NEWS/LENS

- MP wrote a column about the ups and downs of Christmas. Mark, his brother, wrote a guest column.
- Bonnie McCarty, Ike Boling and Philip Baldwin, retiring Justices of the Peace, were honored.

# 1995

## JANUARY

- The first fatality on the SH 35 bypass was recorded. A driver traveling the wrong way had a blood alcohol content of .18.
- SeaAire Furniture moved to Fulton to make way for Bealls in SeaAire Shopping Center. *Eleanor's now occupies the building to which SeaAire Furniture moved.*
- Elementary students vandalized Pirate stadium.
- MP wrote a column advocating that Seafair should be under the auspices of the RFCC. *The RFCC took over Seafair in 2000.*
- Ben Crenshaw and Bill Coore, RCC golf course designers, visited the club.

Ben Crenshaw, second from right, and Bill Coore, right, RCC golf course designers, visited Rockport to consider possible changes to the course.

# 30 YEARS THROUGH THE NEWS/LENS

- ❏ The TMM opened The Museum Store.
- ❏ The 100 Club of AC was formed.
- ❏ DPS Troopers told AC Commissioners the 13' x 13' space they occupied was inadequate.
- ❏ Students were treated and released after their school bus was hit by an 18-wheeler in Holiday Beach.

**FEBRUARY**

- ❏ Free mulch was made available at the AC Transfer Station.
- ❏ The City of Rockport did not receive an anticipated sewer grant for *No Man's Land*.
- ❏ The RFCC unveiled its new tradeshow booth at the Houston Hunting & Fishing Show.
- ❏ The Bank of Corpus Christi, located in Harbor Oaks Village Shopping Center, merged with IBC of Laredo. *Snap Fitness now occupies the space formerly used by the Bank of Corpus Christi.*
- ❏ John Jackson was nominated for the *Academic All-American Hall of Fame*.
- ❏ Plans for the boardwalk at the Demonstration Garden were being made. A path was cleared.
- ❏ Erik Carruth, an RFHS star lineman, signed to play football at Texas Tech.
- ❏ The second fatality on the SH 35 bypass occurred.
- ❏ The 200th person to visit the RFCC Visitors' Center on a given day received a t-shirt.
- ❏ A pistol was seized at RFJH.
- ❏ Alene Mundine filled the seat on the Fulton Town Council left vacant when Ottie, her husband, passed away.

## 1995: YEAR TWELVE

- McDonalds and Taco Bell announced plans to open stores in Rockport.
- Robert Hamilton, a homeowner living in the county, shot and killed an intruder in self-defense.
- Jason Gahan, RFHS senior, was named a National Merit finalist.
- A RFCC breakfast's topic was *The Internet—A Super Highway of Information Just around the Corner.*
- AC Commissioners shuffled HOT funds to allocate 40 percent to dress up Fulton Beach Road.
- The TPWD announced plans to perform dredging work on Cedar Bayou during the summer.
- MP wrote a column about his grandmother turning 90.
- Hu Dat Restaurant opened.

**MARCH**

- Tiger Field opened.
- The ACND approved additional parking for the RFCC and the TMM.

When L.E. Casterline entered an Oyster Shucking Contest he usually won. Here he is pictured with his grandchildren after another first place finish at Oysterfest.

# 30 YEARS THROUGH THE NEWS/LENS

This advertisement for the Cool Coast Camp was uncovered during remodeling of a building in downtown Rockport.

- *Happy Trails* were opened at the Connie Hagar Sanctuary.
- MP wrote a column about selling his first car, a 1984 Honda Accord, which he owned when he got married.
- The ACND approved 10,000 cubic yards of fill/spoil for beach nourishment.
- ACISD Trustees called for a Bond Election to build a new high school. The projected tax increase was 18.9 cents, or about $189 per year, for the average home.
- The mystery of the Austin Street Sawfish was uncovered during remodeling of a downtown Rockport building. *The Cool Coast Camp* was the talk of the town.
- *The Great Texas Trash Off* was a huge success as evidenced by a continual flow of vehicles entering the AC Transfer Station.

## 1995: YEAR TWELVE

### APRIL

- ACND Commissioners voted to change the entity's legal status from a Chapter 62 to Chapter 63 District.
- The third fatality on the SH 35 bypass was recorded. The DPS said it was caused by human error, not the roadway. *At this time, the bypass was only two lanes. The other two-lane portion, making it a divided highway, opened later.*
- The student enrollment of ACISD was reported at 3,206.
- AC Commissioners sought an opinion from the Texas Attorney General regarding dissolving the ACND.
- Former Dallas Cowboy football star Bob Lilly's voice was used in an advertising campaign promoting Rockport-Fulton.
- Austin Street General Store opened.
- MP wrote a column about the Oklahoma City Bombing.

### MAY

- The high school bond election failed 1,620 to 1,118 votes.
- Gary and Nancy Cooper were featured on the cover of *Where to Retire* magazine.
- Country Club Square, a subdivision of patio homes, was being developed at the entrance to RCC.

New banners are placed on the old light standards in downtown Rockport.

# 30 YEARS THROUGH THE NEWS/LENS

- The City of Rockport and AC Clean Team were awarded the *Governor's Community Achievement Award* at the *Keep Texas Beautiful* Convention.
- The Economic Development Corporation received a $5,000 grant from Southwestern Bell.

**JUNE**

- The new *Welcome* signs were dedicated.
- It was learned fifth grade classes would be housed in portable classrooms. More than 100 parents met for an informational meeting at the new Rockport-Fulton Intermediate School.

The welcome sign at the south end of the Copano Bay causeway is one of two still in use.

- To support the Economic Development Corporation, the AC Commissioners gave $10,000, while the ACND contributed $7,500.
- Community leaders participated in a 13-City Discovery Tour.
- Ground was broken on a new McDonalds at SeaAire Shopping Center.
- Debate began regarding the proposed Man Tai Shrimp Farm.
- Nancy Cooper was named *Citizen of the Year* at the RFCC's Annual Banquet.

- The Rockport Benefit Tournament, supporting five charities, was planned at RCC.
- Shirley Burnett, RFHS softball coach, was named *Outstanding High School Softball Coach of the Year.*

City of Rockport officials and AC Clean Team members were ecstatic when they learned Rockport won the Governor's Community Achievement Award in June 1995. It was the first of two such awards won by Rockport, which included $70,000 landscaping awards.

- Ground was broken on the Rockport Retirement Village, consisting of Gulf Point Village and Plaza.

## JULY

- A static display of airplanes at the AC Airport during the July 4 Airshow drew thousands of spectators. E.E. "Dunny" Dunsworth was the key organizer of the airshow.
- The new mural on the Band Shell at Rockport Beach Park was dedicated.
- The Lanfair Lane Colonia Project was funded.
- An Ice Box convenience store clerk was robbed at gunpoint.

# 30 YEARS THROUGH THE NEWS/LENS

- A hotly-contested Holiday Beach Property Owner's Association election was held.
- Bob Pyssen, RFHS athletic director, was hospitalized after being infected by the vibrio virus.
- Bealls opened its doors to record breaking crowds.
- Clark Construction began remodeling the former Oaks Office Park for use as Rockport-Fulton Intermediate School.

## AUGUST

- A female visitor was killed when a bullet, fired accidently while someone was cleaning a gun, hit her as she traveled on Starboard Road.
- A house fire claimed the life of a 12-year-old boy.
- The City of Rockport hired Hernandez and Vargas & Associates for $57,500 to develop a master plan.
- Walston & Adams PC opened. *Bill Walston later became Rockport's City Attorney. Bill Adams was elected AC Judge, and later as AC Court-At-Law Judge.*
- The International Bankshares Corporation - Rockport (IBC) broke ground on its 7,300-square-foot building.
- The RP kicked off its *Power Points Football Contest. The popular contest continues to run today.*
- TPWD's Tom Heffernan retired.

## SEPTEMBER

- Roger Tory Peterson, American naturalist, ornithologist, artist, and educator, dedicated the *Great Texas Coastal Birding Trail* during the HummerBird Celebration at the Connie Hagar Sanctuary Site.
- Dat Nguyen started his first game at Texas A&M. *He would go on to start every game during his four-year Aggie career.*

## 1995: YEAR TWELVE

- The TMM opened the William A. Mann Oral History Center.
- The Fred Hartman Bridge connecting Baytown and LaPorte was opened. *Fred Hartman owned RP, but passed away before the bridge was opened. RP is still owned by members of the Hartman family. MP has worked for the Hartman family his entire career.*

### OCTOBER

- The Hillcrest Addition of Rockport Cemetery opened.

Roger Tory Peterson was in town to dedicate the Great Texas Coastal Birding Trail at the Connie Hagar Cottage Sanctuary site.

- The rebuilt Big Fisherman restaurant reopened. *After reopening and operating for 11 years, the restaurant closed its doors in 2013.*
- James H. Sorenson Jr. was honored for 50 years of working in the banking business.
- Lynn Lee and Joan Sumner opened an artist gallery.
- William Allen and Sue Hastings Taylor were selected to write an Aransas County history book. The book was called, *Aransas: The Life of a Texas Coastal County.*

### NOVEMBER

- The RCA Endowment neared $200,000.

# 30 YEARS THROUGH THE NEWS/LENS

- A manatee, rare for these waters, took a side trip and was spotted in Rockport Harbor.
- A 12-hour music benefit for the Big Tree and Fulton Mansion was held.
- Camper Clinic opened.
- Cactus Pryor, American Broadcaster, was featured at a TMM reception.
- Mindy Durham was named TMM Executive Director.
- A $38,000 Job Training grant was received for an alternative high school.
- George W. Bush, Texas Governor, visited with more than 250 people attending an Ice Cream Social at RCC.
- Five people were killed in a head-on collision on SH 35 N. in Holiday Beach. Both pickups exploded upon impact. Taylor Blocker, who was driving alone at the time, crossed the center line. His blood alcohol content was .283.
- The TMM received a $75,000 Grant from the Sid Richardson Foundation.
- Norman Spears was named ACISD Superintendent.

**DECEMBER**

- Dat Nguyen was named SWC Defensive Newcomer of the Year.
- The Holly Days Festival in downtown Rockport was held to attract shoppers.
- Driftwood RV Haven opened.
- The Rockport City Council approved a patio expansion at the RFCC.
- The Rockport-Fulton YMCA postponed building a permanent structure, due to the YMCA's financial status.

- A fire destroyed the wooden home of Michael and Cathy Hynes.
- The ACEMS Endowment Fund was established to assure future emergency services to Aransas County residents.

# 30 YEARS THROUGH THE NEWS/LENS

## JANUARY

- Four planters in downtown Rockport were destroyed when a motorist lost control of his vehicle.
- Waste Management Inc. bought SW Disposal.
- Birding platforms were placed on Bird Island in the Ski Basin.
- Duffy Oyster proposed *Oyster Landing*, a commercial development at Rockport Beach Park.
- The City of Rockport Park Board approved the concept for a Hike and Bike Trail System.
- An Enhancement Grant was received for the construction of a boardwalk at the Demonstration Garden on Business SH 35.
- Rev. Charles Fake, pastor of First Baptist Church, retired after 31 years of service.

## FEBRUARY

- A fire destroyed the home at 50 Flamingo in Key Allegro.
- More than 100 volunteers participated in the *Winter Texan Trash Off*.
- RP published an editorial noting AC Commissioners made the right decision in not permitting the Man Tai Shrimp Farm to be developed. All other government entities followed suit.
- MP wrote a column calling for no sub-leasing in Rockport Beach Park.
- Rockport Retirement Village opened.

## 1996: YEAR THIRTEEN

- A local pawnshop was burglarized. Police warned citizens that stolen handguns were on the street.
- An IBC robbery suspect was nabbed and the hostage freed minutes after dispatchers received the 911 call.
- MP wrote a column stating the delay in dispatching fire trucks for a fire, which destroyed a Key Allegro home, was unacceptable.
- Oak trees were planted at Connie Hagar Cottage Sanctuary.
- A Fort Worth man downed 192 oysters and won the Men's Oyster Eating contest at Fulton Oysterfest.
- The Rockport City Council approved the City's new Tree Ordinance.
- An RFCC Membership Drive increased membership to 530.
- Bay Breeze Estates was approved for construction, north of Fulton.

### MARCH

- RCC residents spoke against the first phase of the proposed hike and bike route, which would run through that subdivision.
- Larry Sinclair was named the inaugural *100 Club of AC Officer of the Year*.
- *No Man's Land*, or Sylvan Heights, residents filed suit against the City of Rockport and individual council members.
- A winning $63,041 Lotto Ticket was sold at Sunrise Market.
- Glenda Burdick, John Gravell and Eric DeWolfe vied for the position of Rockport Mayor.
- Mark Gilliam and Larry Sinclair were named Community Service Officers by Tim Jayroe, RPD Chief.
- The TMM held its first Mahjong Tourney.

# 30 YEARS THROUGH THE NEWS/LENS

- Residents were split regarding the route for the SH 35 bypass' continuation to the Copano Bay Causeway.

**APRIL**

- A concrete stage was built at the Festival Grounds.
- The plans for the Parade of Palms, paid for with proceeds from the 1995 Governor's Community Achievement Award were revealed. *The Parade of Palms is located along the Business SH 35 median across from the Rockport Ski Basin.*
- Garbage Gobbler provided recycling bins.
- Etcetera, located in front of Bracht Lumber Co., opened.
- Jeff Dinger announced his four-screen theatre would be in operation by summer.
- Justin Spears, RFHS graduate, headed to Fiesta Texas to perform on stage.
- The *March for Parks* attracted walkers to raise funds for the preservation of the Big Tree in Lamar.

**MAY**

- MP wrote a column saying the YMCA would not be constructed in Rockport.
- Jennifer Rice was named *Sportsman of the Year* at the Annual RFHS Sports Banquet.
- The Whooping Crane was named AC's official bird; the Ruby-Throated Hummingbird was named the City of Rockport's official bird; and the Rufous Hummingbird was named the Town of Fulton's official bird.
- *The Texas State Kite Festival* was held at the Rockport Beach Park.
- The Rockport City Council voted against closing a portion of Sabinal Street and the selling of park land, to make way

for a Waffle House to be built next to the proposed Holiday Inn Express. *That park land is now Compass Rose Park.*

## JUNE

- An unidentified murder victim was found in a makeshift grave on Jacoby Lane. Suspect Mark Crawford, former Ingleside Mayor, was the subject of an extensive manhunt, which included appearing on *America's Most Wanted.*
- Jerry Place, former ACSO Chief Deputy, drowned in a diving mishap in the Corpus Christi Ship Channel.
- ACISD Trustees announced plans to repair bleachers at Pirate Stadium, which had been in use for 41 years.
- John P. Jackson was named *Citizen of the Year* at RFCC's Annual Banquet.
- Sacred Heart School broke ground on additional classrooms.
- The TMM received the City of Rockport's support for housing artifacts from the LaSalle Shipwreck.
- The Austwell Aqua Farm hearing was held.

## JULY

- MP wrote a column about flying with Bryan Bracht, local aerobatic pilot.
- Diane Probst, RFCC Executive Director, graduated from the six-year Institute of Organization Management.
- The Rockport City Council approved rezoning for Holiday Inn Express in a 4 to 1 vote.
- ANCO-GSM filed suit against the ACISD.
- Fugitive Mark Crawford was arrested and transported to the AC jail.
- Construction began on the boat ramp and small boat harbor at Cove Harbor North.

# 30 YEARS THROUGH THE NEWS/LENS

The Rockport City Council approved the needed rezoning for the new Holiday Inn Express on a 4-1 vote. That hotel is now an America's Best Value Inn. A newer Holiday Inn Express was built next door.

- The RFCC announced in a press conference it was seeking students for its inaugural Class of Leadership Aransas County.
- A child and a cyclist were killed in separate accidents on Business SH 35.
- Norma Martinez was hired as RP Managing Editor. Her first day on the job was the day Mark Crawford was transported to the AC Jail.

## AUGUST

- MP wrote a column about his family's vacation to Disney World. It was the first time he missed the production of two consecutive newspapers.
- MP was named to the Board of Directors for North Bay Hospital.
- Norwest bought the Rockport location of Victoria Bank & Trust
- The ACISD and Falcon Cable partnered to provide cable in classrooms.
- Hal George was hired as the Attorney for the Town of Fulton. *He continues to serve in that capacity.*
- The property owners of Fulton Outlots requested annexation by Fulton, not Rockport.

**1996: YEAR THIRTEEN**

## SEPTEMBER

- TxDOT doubled the value of the SH 35 Landscaping Award, Parade of Palms, to $72,000.
- The ACISD began distributing security badges.
- IBC opened at its new location.
- Bobby Drennon, longtime RP Bookkeeper, passed away.
- Hummingbird Lodge and Educational Center opened. *It was dissolved in 1999.*
- Fulton Community Church announced that it would build new church facilities.
- Local volunteers helped with the excavation of LaSalle's *LaBelle.*
- The inaugural Leadership Aransas County Class was selected. *Class XVIII graduated in 2014.*

The inaugural Leadership Aransas County class participates in a Challenge Course.

# 30 YEARS THROUGH THE NEWS/LENS

- The AC Airport was awarded a $400,000 TxDOT grant.
- Fuzzy Zoeller, PGA tour pro, filmed one of his fishing shows in local bays.

## OCTOBER

- Tom Lyon of Rockport was the fifth person killed in 1996 in an accident on the SH 35 bypass when he pulled into the path of an 18-wheeler while crossing the highway.
- Rockport's Gospel Force released *The Next Time He Comes*.
- A petition was circulated urging the completion of the SH 35 bypass to include four lanes.
- ABC Learning Center celebrated its 20th Anniversary.
- The City of Rockport unveiled its comprehensive plan.
- An elderly man, who had failed to return to Oak Crest Nursing Center, was found dead at the end of Old Salt Lake Road.
- Betty's Boardwalk was dedicated at the Demonstration Garden.

## NOVEMBER

- The City of Rockport began studying ways to construct a safer intersection where cars enter Key Allegro.
- A delegation from AC traveled to Austin seeking bypass funding.
- The ACISD reported 54 percent of the student population was living in poverty. *As of 2012, 65.3 percent of the student population of ACISD lives in poverty, while 60.4 percent of students residing in the state of Texas live in poverty.*
- A 24-person delegation traveled to Port O'Connor to visit the site of LaSalle's *LaBelle* Excavation.
- The City of Rockport's annexation of Spanish Woods Subdivision and Fulton Outlots was completed.

## 1996: YEAR THIRTEEN

A 24-person delegation visited LaSalle's La Belle excavation site in Matagorda Bay.

- The site of the Aransas Hotel was officially designated a historic site.
- While performing maintenance, two people died inside a septic tank.
- The TMM announced *LaSalle's Texas Odyssey Exhibit* would open.

**DECEMBER**

- Hillary Adams played the piano at Carnegie Hall in New York's Youth Piano Competition.
- Thom Evans, local artist, was selected to design the cover of the new AC History Book.
- Ground was broken for the Holiday Inn Express.
- Jeremy Cessac performed at Carnegie Hall, Paris and the Vatican.
- The Parade of Palms, the palm trees lining the median of

# 30 YEARS THROUGH THE NEWS/LENS

Business Highway 35 across from the Ski Basin, was dedicated.

❏ The *Up With People* Advance Team arrived in Rockport before the organization's inaugural performance.

❏ MP wrote a column about his oldest daughter learning about the true identity of Santa Claus.

The Parade of Palms was developed with funds received from Rockport's first Governor's Community Achievement Award.

# 1997

## JANUARY

- Rockport Properties opened.
- Sherwin Williams opened.
- MP wrote a column about the deaths of John Mitchell and Dr. L.G. Wood.
- Gene Seaman began his service as State Representative for AC.
- The City of Rockport announced a contest to design an official City Flag. A winter Texan won the contest and the $100 prize.
- The RPD bought a SeaDoo Speedster Jet Boat with funds from a Law Enforcement Block Grant.
- The feasibility study for a community pool was approved.
- *Up With People* came to town. Participants made a mark while living with host families as well as through community projects and its performances.

Host families for the cast and crew of Up With People were all smiles when they met their new friends.

# 30 YEARS THROUGH THE NEWS/LENS

- ACCESS Counseling Service opened.

**FEBRUARY**

- Dave Davis retired after 20 seasons at Port Bay Hunting & Fishing Club.
- Cynthia Womack began writing her birding column *Celebrated Feathers* in RP.
- Dr. James Dobson's column, *Focus on Family*, made its debut in RP.
- The City of Rockport hired a firm to collect $500,000 in outstanding warrants and fines.
- The ACND asked the RFCC to return EDC funds. It later rescinded the request.
- Ground was broken on Hunt's Castle.
- The Town of Fulton annexed Fulton Outlots located within its extraterritorial jurisdiction.
- ACISD Trustees approved all-day kindergarten at Rockport Early Childhood Center.
- Coastal Celebration of Lights unveiled its new Christmas Street Decorations.

More than 50 AC residents traveled to Austin for the first AC Day at the Capitol.

# 1997: YEAR FOURTEEN

## MARCH
- Cory Cruser was selected to serve on a future *Up With People* cast.
- More than 50 citizens traveled to Austin for the inaugural Aransas County Day at the Capitol.
- John Witte, former AC Road Administrator, was indicted by an AC Grand Jury on charges of Abuse of Official Capacity.

## APRIL
- Cinema 4 planned its opening with its new three-dimensional sign.

The signs on the front of Cinema 4 are not the same today. The film reel affixed to the building was eventually removed.

- Brian Burks was recognized for saving the life of four-year-old Farren Eddins.
- Lagoon's RV Resort broke ground on its 200 new RV sites.
- Terry Collins opened his law office.
- Aerobatic pilot, Bryan Bracht, proposed to Cheryl Hunter by flying by her in his plane and turning sideways to expose

the words, "Will you marry me?" on the plane's wings. She said "Yes!"

Aerobatic pilot Bryan Bracht proposed to his fiance on a flyby at the AC airport.

- ❏ The 727 prefix was added to the 729 and 790 prefixes for area telephones.
- ❏ Pacific Southwest Bank bought the local Bank of America branch.
- ❏ George Riekers received the *Jefferson Award*, recognizing his years of Volunteerism.
- ❏ AC experienced 22 percent growth since the 1990 U.S. Census, the largest growth by a county in the Coastal Bend.
- ❏ Reavis Wortham's column, *Outdoor Humorist*, debuted in RP.
- ❏ The TMM prepared for its inaugural *Festival of Wines Celebration*.

**MAY**

- ❏ Volunteers built an observation deck at Aransas Woods Birding Site.
- ❏ The RFCC held its inaugural Business Expo.

# 1997: YEAR FOURTEEN

- Cory Reeves won the inaugural *Martha Luigi Choral Music Scholarship*.
- Coldwell Banker Myers-Gallagher opened.
- The Hoopes House opened as a bed and breakfast.
- A left turn signal was installed at the intersection of Business SH 35 and Traylor Boulevard.
- State officials decided to keep the Fulton Mansion under the TPWD's control.
- Gary Autry was selected as RFHS athletic director and head football coach.
- A full-page advertisement regarding the renewal of the Navy's contract at the AC Airport questioned the $27,500 income. AC Commissioners later approved the Navy's Lease.
- The Daughters of the Republic of Texas dedicated the Sparks' Gravesite Marker. *Sparks was one of the last seven survivors at the battle of San Jacinto.*
- McDonalds added 30 seats to meet the demand.

## JUNE

- Holiday Inn Express opened. A fountain honoring John Gimler was dedicated at the site.
- The IBC bank robber was sentenced to serve 12 years in the Texas Department of Corrections.
- MP wrote a column about his daughters going to Girl Scout Camp for the first time.
- Pete Gildon, Rockport City Manager, was fired. Kay Clark was named Interim City Manager.
- The RFCC's inaugural Leadership Aransas County Class graduated 14.
- Glenda Burdick, Rockport Mayor, was elected as one of 16 Texas Municipal League Regional Directors.

# 30 YEARS THROUGH THE NEWS/LENS

- Fully Clingman, Rockport native and former COO of HEB, was keynote speaker at the RFCC Annual Banquet.
- Allen Ray Moers was named *Citizen of the Year* at the RFCC's Annual Banquet.
- Blair Baker, City of Rockport Building Official, was fired.
- Fulton residents organized a Neighborhood Watch Program.
- Formosan termites were discovered in AC.
- RFHS expanded by adding 10 new classrooms.

**JULY**

- Pete Gildon and Blair Baker sought hearings to address their recent firings.
- Father Reese Friedman was named Rector at St. Peter's Episcopal Church.
- A volunteer task force developed a proposal for a Texas State Veterans Health Care Facility.
- AC prepared a new parking lot on the south side of the courthouse in expectation of parking demands during the upcoming trial of former Ingleside Mayor Crawford.
- RP began accepting payment with Visa and MasterCard.
- Larry's Tackle Town was sold to Joe and Janine Stacy.
- Tim Redden and Jay Watkins won the *3rd Annual Saltwater Angler Pro Guides Team Tournament*.
- Due to the failure of the air conditioning system at the district courthouse, Mark Crawford's murder trial was moved to the ACISD Auditorium; costs escalated.
- The AC Clean Team won the *Keep Texas Beautiful Sustained Excellence Award*.
- MP wrote a column calling for a "We Can" Attitude regarding a public swimming pool.

# 1997: YEAR FOURTEEN

- Mark Uhr and Darren Casey, developers, presented a villa concept for waterfront property near the entrance to Key Allegro. *The development never materialized.*
- Gary Autry, RFHS athletic director and head football coach, installed a comprehensive weight program for all football players.
- Ground was broken on the RCA's expansion.
- The Mark Crawford Jury was sequestered. A mistrial was eventually declared.

Employees, board members, and friends of the RCA break ground on the new expanded facilities.

- *Aransas: The Life of a Texas Coastal County* debuted. Zachary Taylor Days was planned.
- Crafts Plus in SeaAire Shopping Center closed its doors.

**AUGUST**
- New banners and planters were installed in downtown Rockport.

# 30 YEARS THROUGH THE NEWS/LENS

- CNN filmed a feature about Dat Nguyen. Bob Pyssen, former RFHS head football coach, was interviewed.
- Ryan McMakin won the gold medal at the National AAU Track Meet.
- A fourth suspicious house fire occurred. A 13-year old juvenile admitted to starting the blaze.
- The EDC's Future Planning Committee met to discuss a conceptual design for the Rockport Waterfront Development.
- Community leaders traveled to Odem to learn about the operation of its public pool.
- Frank Sandoval, owner of Rosita's, was critically injured in a SH 35 bypass accident involving an 18-wheeler.
- J&J Tackle Town, *formerly Larry's Tackle Town*, celebrated its grand opening.
- TxDOT allocated $10.9 million to complete the SH 35 bypass.

**SEPTEMBER**

- Due to new TxDOT regulations, the sign denoting Civic Organizations at the "Y" intersection at SeaAire Shopping was removed.
- *The 10th Annual Fiesta en La Playa* was held.
- RCC made plans for the golf course to receive Audubon Certification.
- Six people were injured in a three-car pileup on

The civic organization sign at the "Y" by SeaAire Shopping Center had to be removed due to new TxDOT regulations.

the SH 35 bypass at Jocelyn Road. *Numerous accidents occurred on the bypass between the opening of the first phase and the second phase, which made it a divided highway.*
- The Mark Crawford murder trial was moved to Bexar County.
- The RFHS Pirate varsity football team beat Taft 19-7, its first win in three-plus seasons.

The Pirate varsity football team won its first game in three-plus years under new Head Coach Gary Autry.

- *Zachary Taylor Days* drew a large crowd.
- The City of Rockport renovated Spencer Park.
- Lisa Baer discovered interesting artifacts under the flooring of the historic Sorenson Store, also known as the Estelle Stair Gallery.

**OCTOBER**
- Seafair was canceled when a storm destroyed tents, disfigured steel poles, and saturated the grounds. *This was the*

beginning of the end of Seafair being operated by the Seafair Organization. The group never recovered financially and turned over operations to the RFCC in 2000.

- *Spirit Columns*, the first piece of public art, was approved by the ACND for a site near Little Bay. The granite piece, created by Jesus Bautista Moroles, was created to honor the volunteer spirit of Jake Colvill and the AC Clean Team. Jane and Bill Mann funded the project.
- MP wrote a column about the need to support the next year's Seafair. *He became involved with Seafair the first year he arrived in Rockport. He ran the crab races for a number of years in the 80s and has organized the races since the RFCC took control of Seafair in 2000.*
- Monroe's warehouse was gutted by fire.
- The City of Rockport refurbished that portion of roadway located within its city limits, commonly referred to as *Fulton Beach Road*.
- Rockport residents opposed allowing manufactured housing being located inside the city limits.
- Walter Knight was named new pastor of the First Baptist Church.
- Christopher Nelson, born with Hunter Syndrome, traveled to Disney World, making his wish come true.

**NOVEMBER**

- The ACND held a grand opening for its new boat launch facility at Cove Harbor.
- The Aransas Woods Bird Sanctuary was dedicated. The Latimer Family donated the property.
- A thief, using a crowbar, robbed the clerk at a Circle K Convenience Store. The suspect was arrested 44 minutes later.

- Pastor Rick Nuffer left Peace Lutheran Church to teach at Concordia Theological Seminary in Fort Wayne, IN.
- A 10-year old Fulton girl was accidentally fatally shot. Her body was dragged to a ditch across the street from the home.
- The remodeling costs of the Saltwater Pavilion was estimated at almost $174,000.

ACND Commissioners officially opened the new boat ramp at Cove Harbor North.

## DECEMBER

- The Rockport-Fulton Christian Community Corps, a part of the Promise Keepers Program, was formed.
- The inaugural Silver Belle Ball grossed $30,000 for the TMM.
- Holly Days and the Celebration of Lights was held. Local children lit the Children's Tree at Rockport Beach Park.
- A Bexar County jury found Mark Crawford, former Ingleside Mayor, not guilty of murder.
- Becky Livingston resigned as secretary to the ACISD Athletic Director after 18 years of service.
- Hunt's Castle opened.
- Lagoons RV Park opened.
- A woman killed her son-in-law during a family fight.
- The ANWR celebrated its 60th Anniversary.

# 30 YEARS THROUGH THE NEWS/LENS

## 1998

The elevated water tower on Enterprise Boulevard shook the ground when it was imploded to make way for the curve in the expanded roadway.

### JANUARY

- The ACISD Bond Election Committee established a hotline. Superintendent Norman Spears answered calls every day from noon until 1 p.m.
- The elevated water tower on Enterprise Boulevard was imploded.
- Sears broke ground for a local retail store.
- Bay Wash Coin Laundry opened.
- New traffic signals were installed at the intersection of the SH 35 bypass and FM 2165.

## 1998: YEAR FIFTEEN

- A proposed nesting site for black skimmers at the Rockport Beach Park was the subject of a public hearing.

**FEBRUARY**

- AC voters approved $14.7 million in School Bonds.
- Almost 500 people attended the grand opening of the RCA's expansion.
- A 30-minute hailstorm hit AC.

**MARCH**

- Two weeks after Jack and Eva Hecker purchased their home in Copano Cove, it was destroyed by a fire.
- O'Reilly Auto Parts and Family Dollar were scheduled to open in SeaAire Shopping Center.
- Lee Maness was hired as the City of Rockport's new City Manager.
- Estelle Stair Gallery held its grand reopening.
- The City of Rockport approved the bylaws and structure of the RFCC's Tourism Development Council.
- Gov. George Bush appointed Glenda Burdick, Rockport Mayor, to the Advisory Commission on State Emergency Communications.

The largest hail storm to hit AC in the past 30 years left piles of hailstones across large portions of AC.

# 30 YEARS THROUGH THE NEWS/LENS

- Mike Henry returned to the City of Rockport as its Building Director.
- Victoria's Gold & Gems planned to move into the former Pacific Southwest Bank building in downtown Rockport.
- The Rockport Rotary Club celebrated its 50th Anniversary.
- A head-on collision on the SH 35 Bypass killed four. Tests showed the presence of alcohol in both drivers.

**APRIL**

- Handmade black skimmer decoys were placed in a proposed nesting site at Rockport Beach Park. *The birds ultimately chose to nest in a different place. As of 2014, the birds nested primarily within the circle drive at the north end of the park.*

Handmade black skimmer decoys were used in an attempt to lure the bird to a particular nesting location at Rockport Beach Park.

- A naked motorcyclist lead police on a chase at 1 a.m.
- RP published an editorial calling for AC Commissioners to tape record their meetings. *To this day, the AC Commissioners do not record their meetings, the only government entity in AC not to do so.*
- The *Spirit Columns* reach skyward and grace the waterfront next to the Ski Basin.

## 1998: YEAR FIFTEEN

- A woman was killed in a one-vehicle rollover on FM 3036.
- Fulton Oysterfest was listed in *Top 200 Events in the Nation*.
- The foundation was poured for the gazebo at Zachary Taylor Park.
- In an early morning blaze, Sacred Heart Church's Knights of Columbus Hall received major heat and smoke damage.
- First United Methodist Church opened First Learning Tree, an educational facility for young children.

Jesus Bautista Moroles stands with Jake Colvill at the dedication of the *Spirit Columns*, AC's first piece of public art.

- A new training facility for ACISD athletics opened. The facility was built with private funds. The flooring was artificial turf from Texas A&M's Kyle Field. *It is still in use today.*
- Texas Historical Commission representatives toured the TMM to analyze the facility for artifacts from La Salle's Shipwreck.
- *Are You Ok?*, a county-wide call system was setup to check on the well-being of residents.

**MAY**

- The Rockport City Council learned about impact fees on developers.

# 30 YEARS THROUGH THE NEWS/LENS

- Shannon Spaulding set a new RFHS record in the 800-meter dash.
- A bird watching platform, built by RFHS students, was dedicated on the property next to McDonalds.
- During the Memorial Day weekend, another accident on the SH 35 bypass sent six to the hospital.
- MP wrote a column about the great duck massacre, when the family dog killed all the pet ducks, except one. The lone survivor, unable to fly, was eventually released into a pond in RCC.

The new ACISD athletic training facility was built with private funds.

## JUNE

- The new Sears Retail Store opened.
- South Rockport Neighbors dedicated the gazebo at Zachary Taylor Park to the City of Rockport.
- The AC Clean Team won its second *Governor's Achievement Award* along with a $70,000 Landscaping Award.
- The Town of Fulton faced a large sewer rate increase from the City of Rockport.
- Norman Spears, ACISD Superintendent, resigned.
- The City of Rockport reported the Saltwater Pavilion Renovations could have a ripple effect in its HOT funding for organizations; primarily a cut in the RFCC's share of those funds.

## 1998: YEAR FIFTEEN

- James Walls was struck and killed by a van, while jogging along Enterprise Boulevard. *This occurred before that street was upgraded to its current condition.*
- Dat Nguyen was on the cover of *Dave Campbell's Texas Football* magazine.
- The ACND rejected the idea for an RCA Sculpture Garden.
- John Krogness was named Administrator of North Bay Hospital in Aransas Pass.
- Rex Littleton retired after 22 years with the City of Rockport.

### JULY

- MP wrote a column about his father surviving a heart attack, which put life in perspective.
- Bahama Bob's opened. The space had been vacant for many years. *The Daily Grind and John Martell's Photography Studio are now at that location.*
- Since understanding population growth in AC was inevitable, a community survey was conducted asking residents about their needs and wants.
- Irma Parker was appointed as Acting City Secretary for the City of Rockport.
- Glenda Burdick, Rockport Mayor, was named *Citizen of the Year* at the RFCC's Annual Banquet.
- The Rockport Sharks Swim Team advanced to the UIL State Swim Meet.
- Rodney Rinche and Abram Rodriguez were lucky to be alive after the car they were in wrapped around a tree in an accident.
- Kay Clark, Rockport City Secretary, was suspended without pay.

# 30 YEARS THROUGH THE NEWS/LENS

- ❏ The TMM's SEA Camp and RCA's Art Link were big hits for the children in AC.
- ❏ The City of Rockport increased its HOT rate from six cents to seven cents.
- ❏ The contract for the expansion of Rockport's Wastewater Treatment Plant was awarded for $1.95 million. The expansion was expected to handle growth for 12 to 15 years.
- ❏ Diane Probst was named one of *10 Texas Women to Watch* at the Business and Professional Women Annual Conference.
- ❏ Agnes A. "Tony" Harden, AC judge, received TxDOT's *Road Hand Award*.
- ❏ Kenneth Callaway, Sr., a Master Fly Caster, produced an instructional video.
- ❏ Charlie Smith won a new truck, boat and trailer after catching a CCA-tagged Redfish.
- ❏ An accident at the intersection of Glass Avenue and Business Highway 35 involved six vehicles and sent 12 to area hospitals. The RP dubbed it "Miracle Monday."

MP dubbed this six-vehicle pileup at the intersection of Business SH 35 and Glass Avenue "Miracle Monday."

- Cementerio San Antonio De Padua, a 103-year-old Cemetery, received a historical marker.
- Dr. Jeremy Mills joined the dentist practice of Dr. Shellenbergar, DDS.
- David Vyoral was hired as AC's Road Engineer.

## AUGUST

- Rick Perry, Republican candidate for Lieutenant Governor, visited Rockport.
- Ryan McMakin won the gold medal in shot put for the second consecutive year at the AAU National Track Meet.
- Tropical Storm Charley missed AC.
- Governor George W. Bush, visiting the area, gave a speech at the Paws and Taws Convention Center.
- The City of Rockport floated $2.5 million in Certificates of Obligation to fund roadwork on Henderson Street and Enterprise and Traylor Boulevards, build a new fire station, make improvements at the Saltwater Pavilion, and purchase a street sweeper.

## SEPTEMBER

- Jim Little, local artist, painted murals on the interior walls of Duck Inn and Pina's Taco House.
- During the Labor Day weekend, large crowds viewed a replica of Christopher Columbus' *La Nina* after it arrived in Rockport Harbor for a one-week stay.
- Several of Sharkey's Employees were No Billed by an AC Grand Jury for Criminal Negligent Homicide after a fatal one-vehicle accident on FM 3036. The driver, who had reportedly been at the bar, had a blood/alcohol level of .20.
- AC had $4.7 million in reserves.

# 30 YEARS THROUGH THE NEWS/LENS

The *La Nina* replica paid a one-week visit, berthing in Rockport Harbor for tours.

- Tom Staley was hired as the new Parks Director, a joint position funded by the City of Rockport and AC.
- MP wrote a column about the need for a permanent funding source for the Countywide Park System.
- The Knights of Columbus Hall reopened after extensive renovations were completed following a fire.

**OCTOBER**

- ACISD Trustees hired a Texas Association of School Boards Consultant to find a new superintendent.
- TxDOT held another public meeting regarding alternative routes for the SH 35 bypass from FM 3036 to the Copano Causeway.
- The City of Rockport explored demolishing eyesores, including the abandoned Charter Foods Building at the corner of Market Street and Business SH 35.

## 1998: YEAR FIFTEEN

- People's Nursing Center opened a new wing at its location on Young Street. *The facility is now called Rockport Coastal Care.*
- Master Gardeners established new planters along Austin Street in downtown Rockport.
- Erik Carruth, Texas Tech and Dat Nguyen, Texas A&M, who were teammates at RFHS, played against each other in a game at Kyle Field.
- The local chapter of Ducks Unlimited raised $65,000, a new record, at its annual banquet.
- Harry Crowe, an employee at the Copano Bay Pier, was shot to death. *To this day no suspect or motive has been found.*

Erik Carruth (77) and Dat Nguyen (9) were teammates at RFHS, and met on the gridiron when Texas Tech played at Texas A&M.

- Hillary Adams, Jeremy Cessac, and Bethanie Henderson performed at New York's Carnegie Hall.

# 30 YEARS THROUGH THE NEWS/LENS

## NOVEMBER

- William Adams was elected Aransas County judge. *Adams was defeated in the 2014 election for county court-at-law judge after his daughter posted a YouTube video showing him beating her with a belt. The video went viral and Rockport received unwanted national attention.*
- Jackie McElroy, a local HEB employee, received that company's *Pinnacle Award*.
- A groundbreaking was held for more construction on the SH 35 bypass.
- Construction of the gazebo at Triangle Park was completed. *Triangle Park is now called Compass Rose Park.*
- Buccaneer Bay Resort in Lamar held its grand opening. *The resort included a refurbished nine-hole golf course. The business is no longer open, but residents continue to play makeshift games on the course.*
- A four-vehicle pileup on the SH 35 bypass killed one.
- The RFHS Pirate varsity football team lost to Edcouch-Elsa in a bi-district game, called *The Mud Bowl*.
- The ACND's new shower facility opened at Rockport Harbor.

## DECEMBER

- A funnel cloud was spotted over AC.
- It was announced the coastal bend area would need to adjust to a new 361 area code. The Austin area kept the 512 area code.
- Gary Autry, RFHS football coach, was named *Coach of the Year*.
- Dat Nguyen won the *Lombardi Award*.
- Agnes A. "Tony" Harden, retiring AC Judge, and Ray Longino,

## 1998: YEAR FIFTEEN

retiring AC Commissioner, were honored at a reception recognizing their years of service to AC.
- A bandit ripped the Express Food Mart's ATM machine off the building.
- A crabber's body was found washed ashore on Key Allegro.
- AC computers were assessed for Y2K problems.
- One man died and six others escaped a mobile home fire on San Antonio Road.

Dat Nguyen, left, won the Lombardi Award at the end of his senior season at Texas A&M.

MP, right, covered the ceremony in Houston.

# 30 YEARS THROUGH THE NEWS/LENS

### JANUARY

- A Rockport man was shot at the intersection of Business SH 35 and Fulton Avenue. Juveniles were taken into custody.
- The Town of Fulton searched for property for a new U. S. Post Office. The current post office is 1,856 square feet with 1,840 boxes. The new post office, proposed by the United States Postal Service, would be 6,500 square feet and have 2,500 boxes. *A new post office in Fulton was never constructed.*
- John and Ruth Lewis donated property in Peninsula Oaks between Lantana and Yucca streets to AC for park use.
- The *River Explorer*, a double barge hotel/cruiser skipped a scheduled stop in Rockport due to inclement weather, which put it behind schedule. Local officials met up with the *River Explorer* in Corpus Christi Harbor.
- *Up With People* came to Rockport for two shows. Host families greeted 150 students from across the globe.
- Dave Segler was named to the *Coastal Bend Coaches Association's Hall of Honor.*
- Ovidio Esquivel, RFHS graduate, was a third-year student at New York City's Julliard School of Performing Arts. *Esquivel now lives in Queens, NY and is an opera singer.*
- The AC Council on Aging considered offering bus services.
- The City of Rockport's Charter Commission looked at paving the way for a possible park taxing entity.

## 1999: YEAR SIXTEEN

- William "Bill" Mann passed away, leaving a legacy of kindness and giving.
- MP wrote a column about how Bill Mann introduced him to Reuben sandwiches at the Key Allegro Yacht Club. *To this day MP enjoys a "good Reuben" whenever possible.*
- James Johnson, a seventh grade teacher, was arrested for indecency with a child.

## FEBRUARY

- A grand opening was held for the new .8 mile nature trail at the Demonstration Garden and Wetlands Pond.
- The Pacific Southwest Bank Community Building was demolished to make way for the new KFC/Taco Bell.
- The City of Rockport stopped the removal of trees on the site of the new KFC/Taco Bell because removal had begun without the approval of a tree plan. *MP alerted the City about the tree removal. A plan, which saved many of the trees from certain removal, was eventually approved.*
- ACISD Trustees broke ground on the new RFMS.
- Dr. Adrain Johnson was hired as the new ACISD Superintendent.
- A woman was killed in a freak accident when her car, traveling at 50 mph, hit a tree near Gordo's Tires.

## MARCH

- The foul smell in Little Bay was due to decomposition of too much vegetation.
- Hank Thompson served as grand marshal of the Oysterfest parade.
- *Dat Nguyen Day* was held in honor of the former RFHS gridiron star and Texas A&M linebacker.

# 30 YEARS THROUGH THE NEWS/LENS

- The second floor of the AC Jail was cleared after a riot.
- A DPS trooper stopped a truck loaded with undocumented workers, 22 ran away. *This continues to be a common occurrence.*
- It was announced new light standards would be installed in the medians in downtown Rockport.
- Construction on RFMS caused changes in traffic patterns.
- Todd Kocian, DPS trooper, was transferred to AC from El Campo. *As of December 2013, Kocian was still stationed in AC.*
- MP was named Hartman Newspaper Inc. *Publisher of the Year.*
- RFHS DECA students finished third, while competing at Nationals for the 18th consecutive year.
- A part of Water Street, prone to tidal flooding, was raised.
- A winning $29,655 Cash 5 Ticket was bought in Rockport.
- North Bay Hospital stopped delivering babies.
- A woman was killed when a Harley Davidson collided with a car on FM 1069.
- ValueBank Texas opened its Rockport branch.
- The ACEMS purchased 12 LIFEPAK units.

**APRIL**

- Shannon Spaulding signed a letter of intent to run track at Texas Tech University.
- The Rockport City Hall Annex opened across the street from City Hall.
- The historical marker for Frandolig Island was dedicated. *Key Allegro is located in the area once known as Frandolig Island.*

## 1999: YEAR SIXTEEN

- Dat Nguyen was drafted by the Dallas Cowboys in the third round with the 85th overall pick.
- Tideflex Valves were installed in south Rockport in an attempt to limit flooding caused during periods of high tide.
- AC Commissioners created a new position to man the new mail room.

### MAY

- A four-year-old Pearsall girl drowned after she was trapped under her family's Carolina Skiff.
- The City of Rockport was designated an official Tree City, USA, the first city in south Texas to receive that designation.
- Puertas and Plantation Shutters opened.
- The Daughters of the Republic of Texas selected Bobby Jackson, RFMS teacher, as the State's *Outstanding Seventh Grade Texas History Teacher of the Year*.
- Threatening graffiti was found at RFHS.
- Two students were sent to juvenile detention facilities after a map they made was found showing sites where bombs were located. The students claimed it was a joke.
- ACISD athletes helped build a garden at the Agricultural Extension Service building.
- The RFHS Campus was quiet when 38 percent of the students were absent due to bomb threats.
- Shannon Spaulding, participating in the 800-meter run, and Matt Pearce, competing in high jump, won gold medals at the UIL State Track Meet.
- All ACND officials were up for reelection.
- AC earned the *Gold Star Safety Award*.

# 30 YEARS THROUGH THE NEWS/LENS

**JUNE**

- Burglars at McDonalds were caught in the act.
- David Rice, RFHS girl's track coach, was named *All South Texas Coach of the Year.*
- Matt Pearce signed a letter of intent in track with the University of Texas.

Almost $3 million was approved for road and drainage work, including curb and gutter on Enterprise Boulevard.

- A new press box was approved for Pirate Stadium.
- A new "Big Blue" Pumper Truck was delivered to the FVFD.
- The ACND approved the concept for a sculpture garden at RCA.
- Van Hovanesian was named *Citizen of the Year* at the RFCC's annual banquet.
- Security Real Estate sold its building, located at Fulton Beach Road and Maple Street, to Southwest Medical Associates, Inc. *The building is again for sale.*

**JULY**

- An open house was held for the renovated Saltwater Pavilion.
- RFHS Choir members left for their *Sound of Music Trip* to Austria and Germany.

## 1999: YEAR SIXTEEN

- The Rockport-Fulton Good Samaritans received a $25,000 grant from the Meadows Foundation.
- The Rockport City Council and AC Commissioners approved $50,000 allocations for a new hike/bike trail.
- Dorothea Montgomery, Castaways founder, was honored.
- Camper Clinic bought additional property on Market and Business SH 35 and began its expansion plan.
- AC Jail inmates escaped from jail and were considered armed and dangerous. *Oklahoma State Troopers captured these inmates in August.*
- Michael Atkinson, sculptor, and Evelyn, his father's widow, unveiled *Man's Best Friend*, the latest piece of outdoor art at the RCA.
- Lee Maness, Rockport City Manager, resigned.

### AUGUST

- Wayne Johnson returned to the ACISD from Beeville to take the helm at RFHS.
- The RFCC established a team to work toward becoming accredited by the U.S. Chamber of Commerce.
- Two ACND Commissioners were ousted in an election, in which all five incumbents faced reelection. Voter turnout was a paltry nine percent.
- MP wrote a column calling for staggered terms for ACND Commissioners.
- Goose Island State Park was ranked *8th Most Visited Park in Texas*.
- Hurricane Brett made a last-minute turn and missed Rockport-Fulton.
- The City of Rockport was awarded a $500,000 TPWD Grant for a public swimming pool.

# 30 YEARS THROUGH THE NEWS/LENS

Powerful Hurricane Brett made an unusual sharp last minute turn and made landfall south of Corpus Christi. A hurricane hasn't severely impacted AC since Hurricane Celia in August 1970.

- Four ACISD campuses received "Recognized" status, while the district received an overall Acceptable Ranking.

**SEPTEMBER**

- A television crew interviewed MP for a story about Dat Nguyen.
- A cement truck, owned by Live Oak Materials, collided with a car and three were sent to the hospital.
- Walter Hill was hired again to serve as Rockport's Interim City Manager.
- Margaret Rust, philanthropist and Kent Ulberg, sculptor, announced their collaboration for the first piece of outdoor art for the RCA Sculpture Garden. *The sculpture, Rites of Spring, displays a pair of Whooping Cranes.*
- Support was needed for land for a new Fulton Post Office location.

## 1999: YEAR SIXTEEN

- The last day to use the 512 area code was Sept. 17, 1999. *The area code, 361, went into effect.*
- AC Commissioners urged the DPS to man a local driver's license office.
- The AC Clean Team hosted a *Keep Texas Beautiful Training Conference*.
- The picture of a mobile home fire was the first color picture published in RP.
- An 18-wheeler turned over at the intersection of the SH 35 bypass and FM 3036, spilling its load of drilling pipe.
- A rusted, sunken boat at the entrance to Rockport Harbor was removed.
- A head-on accident on the SH 35 bypass at Murphy Road injured two.
- Pacific Southwest Bank was purchased by First Capital Bank.

A rusted sunken tugboat, which had been at the entrance of Rockport Harbor for 30-plus years, was removed.

# 30 YEARS THROUGH THE NEWS/LENS

## OCTOBER

- The driver of a dump truck spilled the truck's load after turning over at the intersection of the SH 35 bypass and FM 3036.
- William Mays was hired as ACND Counsel.
- Students from Texas A&M studied the erosion problem on Key Allegro.

Major accidents, including multiple fatalities, were the norm on the SH 35 bypass when it was only two lanes.

- Sam Zapata was hired as the new ACISD Police Chief.
- ACISD Trustees considered allowing employees to donate sick leave to those who may need additional sick leave.
- A Parks Plan for AC began to take shape.
- An automobile accident claimed the life of one, while fire destroyed a home, leaving one in critical condition.
- The RFHS Pirate varsity football team beat Gregory-Portland for the second straight year, an accomplishment, which hadn't occurred for many years.

# 1999: YEAR SIXTEEN

- A TABC hearing was held to determine the fate of Chances Nightclub's Liquor License.
- Angie Ruddock and Danny Adams II were named co *Sportsmen of the Year* at the Ducks Unlimited Banquet.
- Western Auto closed its doors after a 35-year run. *The building still remains in downtown Rockport, most recently housing the Flying Pig Emporium and is now for lease.*

## NOVEMBER

- Cape Velero Residents agreed to pay a little more than $15,000 for road renovations.
- The City of Rockport hired Thomas Blazek, the City Manager of Port Lavaca, as its new city manager.
- Martha Luigi, 60, beloved RFHS choral director, passed away after losing her battle with cancer.
- Following an accident on FM 1069, a mother and her daughter were killed after being thrown from their vehicle.
- Kathy Roberts-Douglass was hired as the TMM's new Executive Director.
- The new street lights in downtown Rockport were lit.
- The *MV Pisces* sunk in Rockport Harbor after safely returning students, who were on a trip.

The new antique streetlights on Austin Street in downtown Rockport introduced a new look.

# 30 YEARS THROUGH THE NEWS/LENS

The *MV Pisces* sank in Rockport Harbor, after returning passengers to safety.

- An oil well explosion in the back section of American Adventure RV Park injured four.
- Three students from the Rockport-Fulton area were directly affected by the tragic collapse of the Aggie bonfire.

**DECEMBER**

- The Speedy Stop in Lamar was deliberately set on fire and was closed for a short period of time.
- MP wrote a column under the headline, "It was a Different Kind of Football Game," which focused on his experience on the sidelines of the Aggie/Longhorn Game following the collapse of the Aggie Bonfire. *The Aggies, playing on pure emotion, beat the highly ranked Longhorns.*
- Because it was insulated with asbestos, Dr. Wood's old office building was demolished.

## JANUARY

- After a knifepoint holdup, the bandit fled from Speedy Stop on Business SH 35 S.
- David Petrusaitis, incumbent Sheriff, fired Stan Bynum, ACSO Investigator, when Bynum filed to run against him in the upcoming election.
- New Year's Day came and went with few Y2K glitches.
- ACND Commissioners approved a parking ordinance for Cove Harbor.
- The RFCC's Chinese Auction was renamed *Awesome Auction* in its 20th year.
- Security Real Estate celebrated its grand opening at a new location.
- A judge recommended allowing an alcohol permit for Chances Nightclub on the SH 35 bypass.
- Howard Foster, 65, was found guilty of the murder of Judith Lackey, 59, and was sentenced to 20 years in prison.
- A woman driving the wrong way on the SH 35 bypass caused an accident at the bypass' intersection with FM 2165. Mai Nguyen, 35 of Rockport, was killed, and seven others were sent to area hospitals.
- A rose garden was planned for the Fulton Mansion.
- Kelly Gibson was promoted to General Manager of RP.
- A new rule stopped the rental of personal watercraft in the ski basin.

# 30 YEARS THROUGH THE NEWS/LENS

The Big Tree in Lamar receives one of its bi-annual trims.

- Ten additional acres were purchased by the City of Rockport and added to Memorial Park.
- Norma Martinez was promoted to Managing Editor of RP.
- A $573,638 grant was received from the Texas Transportation Commission for the Tule Hike and Bike Trail.

**FEBRUARY**

- Laney Bardin received a full scholarship to play volleyball at Texas A&M-Corpus Christi.
- The AC Senior Services Center announced its expansion.
- The local chapter of Habitat for Humanity broke ground for its first home.
- A construction worker at RFMS was injured after falling 30 feet and landing on concrete.
- A meeting was held about the possible formation of a Green Party of the Coastal Bend.

Ground was broken on Habitat for Humanity's first home in AC in February 2000.

- The FVFD purchased new Jaws of Life equipment.
- The DPS Driver's License Office was relocated to Aransas Pass by mutual agreement.
- The AC Humane Society, facing reduction in services, reported that additional volunteers were needed at its shelter.

## MARCH

- A Corpus Christi woman died in a rollover accident on the SH 35 bypass.
- John Roaten received an appointment to West Point.
- Law enforcement agencies sought information about person(s) shooting at cars on the SH 35 bypass.
- The AC Airport was touted by *Texas County Progress* as one of the two best-managed airports in the state.
- An AC Jail inmate walked out of jail, but was nabbed immediately by the jail administrator, who was outside overseeing work being done by jail trustees.
- Mark Gilliam won the Republican Primary for AC Sheriff. Joaquin Martinez won the Democratic Primary.
- Kathy Barnes was named Principal of Sacred Heart School.

# 30 YEARS THROUGH THE NEWS/LENS

- Debbie Shedden, RFJH Teacher, was named *Outstanding Teacher in the Region*.
- John Wendell, retired AC Judge, died of heart attack.
- Lewis Park, located on Griffith Drive, was dedicated and offers an open play area and picnic sites.
- Benny McLester was injured and a Corpus Christi man was killed in an accident on the SH 35 bypass.

**APRIL**

- RFMS eight graders helped kick off a Storm Drain Stenciling Program, which involved labeling storm drain inlets with slogans or warnings to remind citizens not to dump pollutants into the drains, which flow into the bays.
- The ACND bought new VHF radio equipment to communicate with boat traffic.
- The ACMSI celebrated its 25th anniversary. *The Little Old Ladies in Tennis Shoes* began raising funds for the local EMS when the ACMSI was formed in 1975. *The ACMSI was disbanded in 2008*.
- MP wrote a column about the legacy being built by *The Little Old Ladies in Tennis Shoes*.
- "Rock Art" had a new meaning as cement rocks were used in the construction of the RCA's Sculpture Garden.
- Allen Ray Moers stepped down after chairing the RFCC's Spring Fling Outdoor Media event for 15 years.

RFMS students joined with Rockport Mayor Glenda Burdick in the Storm Drain Stenciling Program.

## 2000: YEAR SEVENTEEN

- Emily Rice signed a letter of intent to run cross-country and track at Texas A&M-Corpus Christi.
- Chances Nightclub opened. *The building on the SH 35 bypass is now vacant.*
- The RFCC was "Accredited" by the U.S. Chamber of Commerce. Past chairmen were recognized during a celebration at the Saltwater Pavilion.
- The RFCC took control of Rockport Seafair.
- ACND Commissioners approved a set of rules under which they would operate in future meetings.
- The City of Rockport bought H&S Water Company and heard customers' pleas to waive the $50 deposit.
- Construction workers placed brick pavers at the intersection of Business SH 35 and Loop 70 as part of $70,000 Landscape Project earned by winning the *Governor's Community Achievement Award.*

**MAY**

- Dr. Paul Hamilton, psychologist, opened his practice.
- Wilson McBride was hired as new ACND Harbor Superintendent.
- The USPS said possible construction of a new Fulton Post Office was being deferred.
- A call for donations was made to offset the $345,000 shortfall of the public pool.
- Glenda Burdick was reelected Mayor with 85 percent of the vote.
- MP wrote a column saying a change in the ACND Dollar Leases should not be considered.
- A $2.6 million Road Improvement and Drainage Project on Omohundro Street near RFHS was announced.

# 30 YEARS THROUGH THE NEWS/LENS

- ACISD announced that a new Little Bay Elementary would open in the fall.
- Clay Gillis, former ACISD business manager, was one of six killed in a tragic plane crash at Houston's Hobby Airport.
- MP wrote a column about his good friend, Clay Gillis. *Gillis' daughters babysat MP's daughters and he would always say, "Just wait Probst...your time is coming."*
- Larry's Sharpening & Repair opened.
- Joey Albin, RFJH seventh grader, received National Recognition from Duke University when his ACT score was ranked in the top 18 percent of seniors.
- Property appraisals increased between eight and 12 percent.

**JUNE**

- AC Commissioners approved the construction of a new administrative building at the AC Airport.

The home side of Pirate Stadium received new bleachers in 2000.

## 2000: YEAR SEVENTEEN

- TxDOT announced bids on highway improvement projects would be let sooner than expected.
- A proposed welcome billboard sign highlighting Dat Nguyen was turned down by the Rockport City Council.
- E.E. "Dunny" Dunsworth attended the GOP National Convention, making a long-time dream come true.
- New bleachers were delivered to Pirate Stadium, but couldn't be installed until the old seats were demolished.
- Kay Barnebey was the 2000 Art Festival Poster Artist.
- An Aransas Pass man was struck and killed on the SH 35 bypass in a hit and run.
- Valerie Guillory was named *Citizen of the Year* at the RFCC's Annual Banquet.
- Darlene Locke, AC Extension Agent, was named *Friend of 4-H*.
- Green Acres was formed.

**JULY**

- Neighbors opposed the proposed site of the new HEB.
- The Rockport City Council approved a new animal control ordinance.
- Plans to extend the Memorial Park Hike and Bike Trail began.
- Sara Jackson and Jeanne Travis performed with *Up With People*. Due to that organization's financial problems during the tour, the young women returned home.
- Tobacco Express opened.
- A brush fire off Old Salt Lake Road burned 70 acres of land; many homes were saved.
- Louise Wilken, longtime Democratic party chairman, was honored for her service.

# 30 YEARS THROUGH THE NEWS/LENS

- The traffic signal at Business SH 35 and Colorado Street was installed.
- The ACND unveiled its final draft of the Rockport Harbor Traffic Plan.
- The TPWD held *Fish Fest 2000* in honor of Joe Martin, Marine Biologist who drowned in 1993.

**AUGUST**

- The owner of KT's Grocery shared his concerns with the Fulton Town Council about parking issues in downtown Fulton.
- The new SH 188, between Rockport and Sinton, opened.
- New traffic signals were installed at Business SH 35 and Enterprise Boulevard.
- The AC budget had an $800,000 shortfall.
- A shootout in Holiday Beach ended with the death of a 20-year-old.
- A water leak ruined the RFJH gym floor. *It is now known as the RFHS Gold Gym.*
- Rene Reynaldo Gonzales, 21, of Rockport was killed in a rollover accident on Fulton Beach Road, or Broadway Street, at the bridge crossing the canal entrance to Harbor Oaks.
- Certified Auto opened.
- Kline's Cafe was under new ownership. Garrett Gill reopened the iconic restaurant with a new menu. Winery By the Bay is now located there.

**SEPTEMBER**

- An AC Jail inmate attempted to hang himself.
- The AC Clean Team changed its name to *Keep Aransas County Beautiful*.

## 2000: YEAR SEVENTEEN

- A patrolman, whose attention was diverted, caused a three-car pile up; no injuries were reported.
- Martin De Leon, Precinct 1 Justice of the Peace, filed for an increase in mileage allowance.
- MP wrote a column about the misadventures of those who sailed on the maiden voyage of the *Texas Treasure* Casino Boat.
- Tom Blazek, Rockport City Manager, said the proposed public pool was not a City of Rockport Pool and all parties needed to be on board to fund the pool's operations.
- *Rites of Spring*, a sculpture of a pair of Whooping Cranes by Kent Ulberg, was unveiled. It was the first piece of art dedicated in the RCA's Sculpture Garden.
- After adults were alerted by an eight-year-old, an 11-year-old was rescued from a drainage pipe.
- David Dewhurst, General Land Office Commissioner, was in town to discuss erosion issues.
- The *Dat Nguyen Welcome Sign* was dedicated in Fulton. MP was master of ceremonies. The Rockport City Council did not allow

*Rites of Spring* was the first piece of art dedicated in the RCA Sculpture Garden.

# 30 YEARS THROUGH THE NEWS/LENS

*the sign, while the Fulton Town Council approved the sign.*

❏ The new RFMS was dedicated before a huge crowd.

❏ The Town of Fulton began looking at speed bumps as means to slow traffic.

**OCTOBER**

❏ Four rare Australian black swans were spotted in Little Bay.

❏ The AC Jail had areas of non-compliance for the second consecutive year.

❏ A five-vehicle accident on the SH 35 bypass sent two to the hospital.

The Dat Nguyen Welcome Sign was dedicated on SH 35 in Fulton.

❏ The new Jehovah's Witness Kingdom Hall was constructed in four days.

❏ The *Up With People* advance team arrived. Achiko Hayashi of Japan stayed with MP's family.

❏ Kathleen Akin was honored with the *Governor's Yellow Rose of Texas Award*. This award honors women for their significant contributions to their communities and Texas in the preservation of Texas History.

## 2000: YEAR SEVENTEEN

- Seafair, the first year under RFCC operation, experienced an almost total rainout.
- ACISD Trustees agreed to pay the school's share of maintenance costs for the new public swimming pool.
- The *Vietnam Veterans Moving Wall* arrived in Rockport.

The *Vietnam Veterans Moving Wall* was set up for four days.

- A Houston fisherman was critically injured when thrown from a boat.
- Gary Swenchonis, Jr., RFHS class of '94, was missing after terrorist attack on the USS Cole. *Swenchonis was later confirmed killed in the attack. He received the Purple Heart posthumously.*
- Family, friends, and students gathered at the Saltwater Pool to dedicate benches in honor of Anita Dingenary, teacher, softball coach and member of Sacred Heart Catholic Church, who passed away.

# 30 YEARS THROUGH THE NEWS/LENS

- The ACISD Auditorium was rededicated and renamed in memory of Martha Luigi, long time choral director.
- A new building for early voting opened at 502 E. Concho St.
- David Pilgrim was named *Ducks Unlimited Conservator of the Year*.
- Another accident on the SH 35 bypass injured two.
- Jackie Bauer won an all-expense paid trip to Las Vegas from Radio Station 104.5, The Plant.
- The *Music of the Sea Festival* was held at the TMM.

## NOVEMBER

- Two were injured in a three-car pileup on the SH 35 bypass.
- The U.S. Coast Guard was sent to Fulton Harbor for a morning diesel spill.
- Mark Gilliam, AC Sheriff, garnered 72 percent of the vote in the election for AC Sheriff.
- Pam Heard unseated Mary Sherman, incumbent District Clerk.
- The buildings for Rockport Printing and the new Dairy Queen were under construction.
- The RFHS Pirate varsity football team finished the regular season 10-0.
- The TMM broke ground on the Lighthouse Project.
- HEB confirmed its purchase of Palo Alto RV Park for a new super store.
- A Rockport man crashed his helicopter in Aransas Bay, but escaped unhurt.

## DECEMBER

- The RFHS Pirate varsity football team lost to Calallen 16-39 in the quarterfinals.

## 2000: YEAR SEVENTEEN

The Pirates lost to Calallen in the quarterfinals, ending a spectacular 13-1 season.

- An online poll in RP showed 56 percent of respondents were okay with $1 ACND Leases for non-profit organizations.
- The groundbreaking for the new public pool was postponed.
- A fire gutted Rudder's Bar and Grill in downtown Rockport's Austin Street Station.
- Sea Mist Townhomes, located on FM 3036, opened.

# 30 YEARS THROUGH THE NEWS/LENS

## JANUARY

- Walmart received a bomb threat.
- Jimmy Luigi formed the Coastal Bend Orchestra and performed at RCA.
- Jerry Wendell, 75, father of the Wendell Family Fireworks, passed away. A fireworks tribute was held in his honor.
- RP began accepting Visa, MasterCard, and Discover for bill payment.
- The first Habitat for Humanity home was dedicated.
- The ACND signed a 50-year lease with the TMM.
- New speed humps in Fulton began impacting unsuspecting drivers.

Ground is broken on the new Community Swimming Pool.

## 2001: YEAR EIGHTEEN

Rockport Beach Park was the first beach in Texas to receive the Blue Wave Beach designation.

- RP began inserting *American Profile* in its Weekend Edition.
- Ground was broken on a new public swimming pool.
- The Rockport Beach received the first Blue Wave Beach status in Texas.
- A handgun was found in a backpack at RFHS.

**FEBRUARY**

- A DPS trooper wounded a man to end a standoff. Dennis Wooten was charged with attempted capital murder.
- The *La Belle: Desolate Voyage Exhibit* opened at TMM.
- The TMM's model of LaSalle's *La Belle*, funded by George and Sara Yamini, was unveiled.
- MP wrote a column about the experience of "tagging along" during a drug raid.
- Jacob Scott signed a letter of intent to play football for Texas A&M-Kingsville
- Latitudes Restaurant opened.

# 30 YEARS THROUGH THE NEWS/LENS

- A yacht owned by a Houston man was destroyed in a fire at the Key Allegro Marina.
- A local Kiwanis Club was formed.
- Rockport Mail Center moved to its new location in Rockport Plaza.
- Dave Segler, former RFHS Coach, was inducted into the *Gateway to Mexico All-Sports Clinic Hall of Honor.*
- Angelina Lara Flores, 55, was killed in an accident at the intersection of the SH 35 bypass and FM 2165.
- The AC Airport received a $1.9 million grant to upgrade facilities.

**MARCH**

- Johnny Rodriguez was the Grand Marshal of the Oysterfest Parade.
- RP published its inaugural Historical Marker Guide.
- Concerned parents sought a bullying policy at an ACISD Board Meeting.
- The Town of Fulton made plans to bulkhead the shoreline.
- Lynn Johnson Realty opened.
- Gary Autry, RFHS athletic director and head football coach, resigned to accept a job closer to his Arkansas home.
- Jobeth Mixon, 74, a former RFHS teacher, was killed in an accident at the intersection of the SH 35 bypass and FM 2165.
- An infant passenger, in a car parked on the shoulder of the SH 35 bypass, was killed when another car struck the parked car. This was the third death on the SH 35 bypass in 30 days.
- MP wrote a column about drivers' roles in SH 35 bypass

## 2001: YEAR EIGHTEEN

accidents even though the bypass was not yet a divided highway.
- Ray O'Brien, former Rockport Mayor, passed away after a short battle with cancer.
- The Rockport City Council considered placing up to five amendments on the May 5 Charter Election ballot.
- Dr. Jerry Shaw, Anita Dingenary and Clay Gillis were honored during the Opening Day Ceremony at Rockport-Fulton Little League.

### APRIL
- Pizza Hut, Hemingway's, First Baptist Church, and IBC Bank were under construction.
- Glenda Burdick, Rockport Mayor, made a public statement about annexation issues and personal attacks.
- Johnny Mac Hollinger was hired as RFHS' new athletic director and head football coach.
- An RFMS student was suspended for threatening to burn down the school.
- A circus benefitting the ACEMS Building Fund came to town.
- The Holiday Beach Volunteer Fire Department (HBVFD) signed a contract to build a new fire station. *Construction on the station was never completed and the HBFD eventually merged with the Lamar VFD.*
- The inaugural Tejano Festival was held at Fulton Navigation Park. *It is no longer held.*
- Hillis Dominguez, after 22 years of service as an ACND Commissioner, resigned due to illness.
- Bryan White, country singing sensation, attended the RFCC's Spring Fling.

# 30 YEARS THROUGH THE NEWS/LENS

Bryan White, second from right, attended RFCC's Spring Fling Outdoor Media Event. He is the son-in-law of Dave and Cindy Colmer.

- Town of Fulton officials and family members of Wanda Rouquette Sparks dedicated a live oak tree in her honor on the grounds of old Fulton Schoolhouse.
- The second Habitat for Humanity Home was built with funds from the local Lions Club and Lions Club International.

**MAY**

- Rick McLester received the Jefferson Award for his leadership and community service for the local Little League's Challenger Division.
- A large cinder block was thrown from the SH 35 bypass overpass at FM 1069, shattering a passing car's windshield and just missing the driver.
- City Charter Amendments calling for new annexation and deannexation rules were defeated at the polls.
- Sabrina Moreno, 21, was found dead, floating near the Degussa Plant's company docks. Two Aransas Pass men were arrested in connection with her murder.
- The ACISD sold property to Walmart to clear the way for a new Walmart Supercenter.

A bench at Veterans Memorial Park was dedicated in memory of Gary Swenchonis Jr. who was killed in the USS Cole terrorist attack.

- Samantha Spaulding set a new school record in 300-meter-hurdles at the UIL State Track Meet.
- Kim Arambula received minor injuries, after a cinder block thrown from the SH 35 bypass overpass at FM 1069, landed in her lap.
- A fire gutted the Boiling Pot Restaurant before the Memorial Day weekend.
- A bench was dedicated to the memory of Gary Swenchonis, Jr., a local sailor killed in the USS Cole Terrorist Attack.

**JUNE**

- A new County Court-At-Law was a possibility in AC thanks to a new state law.
- A bench at the AC Courthouse was dedicated in memory of John Wendell, former AC Judge.

# 30 YEARS THROUGH THE NEWS/LENS

- Oscar Pina, AC Commissioner, Janet, his wife, and Jeramie, his son, filed a lawsuit against the City of Rockport and the ACND as a result of injuries sustained by Jamie in a diving accident in the Saltwater Pool.
- The ACND approved an ordinance allowing people to live on board their boats in Rockport Harbor.
- *Sweet Six* produced their first Gospel recording.
- Dr. Nichole Soto purchased 20/20 Optical.
- The body of Theo Khamphoumy, 47, a shrimper, was found washed ashore on Key Allegro after his boat sank in a storm.
- MP wrote a column about the death of his college roommate's infant daughter, who was found dead in the family car.
- Jack Daniels, Rockport Rotarian, was Rotary District Governor.
- Penny Baldwin, ACISD teacher, was named *Citizen of the Year* at the RFCC's annual banquet.
- The Rockport-Fulton Good Samaritans broke ground on its new $100,000 facility.
- MP wrote a column about the need for a proper business zoning buffer on the property between FM 3036 and the north boundary of Rockport Country Club. *The Rockport City Council did not approve a developer's proposed business rezoning request because he failed to provide information about who would operate on the rezoned property.*
- MP wrote a column about his families' first cruise. *The Carnival Triumph, the ship on which they cruised, is the same one, which had to be towed back to shore, and was the subject of national news in 2013.*

**JULY**

- A stealth bomber impressed the crowd at the airshow.

## 2001: YEAR EIGHTEEN

The extension of the Memorial Park Hike and Bike Trail is dedicated.

The ACISD Education Foundation was formed in August 2001.

- Kathie Holbrook was hired as new aquatics swim coach by the City of Rockport and the ACISD.
- Larry Ellis, a lone resident, initially spoke out against HEB's decision to build at the Palo Alto RV site.
- RP hosted an open house for its remodeled facilities.
- Marty Cantu was named postmaster at Rockport Post Office.

**AUGUST**

- Wayne Johnson was selected new ACISD Superintendent after Dr. Adrain Johnson resigned.
- A fire at the American GI Forum caused heavy damages.
- The extension of the Memorial Park Hike and Bike Trail was dedicated.

# 30 YEARS THROUGH THE NEWS/LENS

- The ACISD Education Foundation was formed.
- Eric Lower, co-owner of Hunt's Castle, was found shot dead on one of the hotel's walkways.
- New population signs were installed. Rockport boasted 7,385 residents, while Fulton announced 1,553 residents. *In 2013, AC had an estimated population of 24,356.*
- Phillip Savoy, taxi driver, was stabbed and his taxicab was stolen.
- The Rockport Area Association of Realtors opened a new office in Market Center, next to Rockport City Hall.

**SEPTEMBER**

- A traffic signal at Stadium Drive and Enterprise Boulevard was installed. *This was the first traffic signal installed and funded by the City of Rockport.*
- A one-block portion of Broadway Street in Fulton, between Fulton Beach Road and Casterline Drive, was renamed Rouquette and Wendell Boulevard.
- AC residents awoke on a Tuesday morning to hear the tragic news about the 9-11 terrorist attacks on the United States.
- MP wrote a column under the headline, "Core of American Conscience Hit Hard."
- Charter Bank announced it would open a Rockport branch at the former site of Olympic Savings.
- The collapse of a section of the Queen Isabella Causeway, connecting Port Isabel and South Padre Island, involved a local tugboat.
- TxDOT announced work to complete the bypass as designed, a four-lane divided highway, should begin by the end of the year.

## 2001: YEAR EIGHTEEN

- The City of Rockport faced a mold problem at the police station.
- The Band Shell at Rockport Beach Park was repainted.

**OCTOBER**

- Aranzazu Restaurant opened across from Harbor Oaks Village Shopping Center. *Aranda's Mexican Grill is now located there.*
- Construction on the Children's Discovery Garden at Green Acres began.
- Rockport Seafair, operated by RFCC, made a dramatic comeback after being washed out by heavy thunderstorms the previous year.
- The Angel Rose Inn, a bed and breakfast, opened.
- A large contingent of San Antonio Media was in town covering the trial of Salvadoran Nelson Escolero, who was on trial for kidnapping Catholic Archbishop Patrick Flores.
- Descendants of the Davidson family, who lived in the Fulton Mansion after George Fulton, toured the home.

The Community Aquatic Park officially opened in October 2001. Ceil Frost was a major private contributor for the project.

# 30 YEARS THROUGH THE NEWS/LENS

- The Community Aquatic Park opened.
- A kayak race from the Rockport Beach Park to Port Aransas was held as part of the *Lone Star Legacy Weekend*.
- Fun Times Skating Rink opened in Encina Plaza. *The rink is now closed.*
- Drug dogs did not find any drugs during a clean sweep of a few ACISD campuses.
- Pianists Michael Heil, Jas Nowicki, Hillary Adams, and Christopher Beavers performed at Carnegie Hall in NYC.
- ABC Learning Center celebrated its 25th Anniversary.
- A new traffic signal was installed at the intersection of Business SH 35 and FM 3036.
- Joni Luna, RFHS volleyball coach, was named *District Coach of the Year*, while Cody Birk was selected *MVP*.
- The RFCC and the AC Historical Commission developed a historical, narrated walking tour. *Similar walking tours of homes will be offered by the History Center for Aransas County.*

**NOVEMBER**

- The ACISD Education Foundation kicked off its Founders' Drive and 85 percent of the $100,000 goal was achieved.
- Gulf Pointe Plaza opened.
- The Town of Fulton held a future planning session attended by a full room of residents, who wanted to discuss future growth.

**DECEMBER**

- Derrick Construction crews installed new breakwaters at the entrance to Leggett Light Channel.

## 2001: YEAR EIGHTEEN

- The Corpus Christi Orchestra and the RFHS Choir performed in the inaugural Holiday Symphony by the Sea. Cory Reeves, RFHS graduate, was guest conductor.
- Chris Nelson, 11, collected can tabs to raise funds for Hunter's Syndrome, a disease from which he suffered. A soldier donated a duffel bag full of tabs to Nelson. He eventually gathered two million tabs raising $5,400. Fellow students said four million can tabs were now a possibility. *Nelson passed away on July 5, 2014.*
- The District Clerk's Office began Passport Service in AC.
- Brenda and Ross McElwee filed a Title IX Complaint seeking equality for girls sports.
- Joan and Lynn Lee created a Charitable Remainder Trust to benefit the RCA.

# 30 YEARS THROUGH THE NEWS/LENS

## JANUARY

- Horizon Veterinary Clinic opened.
- North Bay Hospital was sold to American MedTrust.
- The ACISD Education Foundation presented $32,000 to teachers to fund 12 grants. *Since its inception, the foundation has provided more than $1 million in grants, scholarships and special programs that directly impact students' education in the ACISD.*
- Holy Cross Lutheran Church on FM 1781 was dedicated.
- The Genealogical Society for AC was formed.
- One person was fired and four resigned from the AC Jail following allegations a female inmate became pregnant, while serving time.
- The RVFD's new central fire station was dedicated. The building cost $650,000.

RFVD's new central fire station is dedicated.

- ACISD Trustees approved these grade changes at the following elementary schools: Little Bay: Pre-kindergarten - Kindergarten; Live Oak: Grades 1-3; Fulton: Grades 4-5.

**FEBRUARY**
- AC Commissioners leased Tiger Field to the ACISD.
- Norvell Ford Jackson Sr., 86, lifelong Rockport resident and businessman, passed away.
- MP wrote a column under the headline "Time is Right for Joint Law Enforcement Center".
- Logan Respess was hired as new AC Agricultural Extension Agent.
- Wilson McBride, ACND Harbormaster, was honored by AC Commissioners for his work in securing erosion grants.
- HEB agreed to pay $94,000 for the installation of a turning lane in front of its new store on Business SH 35.

**MARCH**
- Oysterfest officials began offering a shuttle program to help remedy the parking problems during the festival.
- Glenn Guillory defeated Larry Barnebey in the GOP Primary for AC Judge.

The RFVD's old station was demolished as soon as the new station was opened.

# 30 YEARS THROUGH THE NEWS/LENS

The new location of the Rockport-Fulton Good Samaritan Center on S. Ann Street is dedicated.

- The old RVFD Station was demolished.
- The RPD moved to temporary quarters to escape mold problems.
- The Rockport-Fulton Good Samaritan Center opened on S. Ann Street.
- Simon Michael, artist, instructor, philosopher, and poet, died at the age of 96.
- Aransas First asked the Rockport City Council for permission to use a portion of 12th Street as a parking area for the Bird Sanctuary at Cove Harbor.
- The Annual 4th of July Airshow was canceled due to construction at the AC Airport.

**APRIL**
- Danny Adams defeated Asa Yeamans in the Precinct 3 County Commissioner GOP Primary Runoff Election.
- Howard Murph defeated Darren Sigwald in the Precinct 4 County Commissioner GOP Primary Runoff Election.

## 2002: YEAR NINETEEN

- ACISD Trustees changed the Gifted/Talented Program after realigning elementary campuses.
- The First Baptist Church on Enterprise Boulevard was dedicated.
- The RFHS Lady Pirate varsity track team won the UIL District Track Championship for the fourth consecutive year.
- Dat Nguyen signed a six-year, $13 million contract with the Dallas Cowboys.
- Jon Shaw and Charles, his son, were recognized for saving the lives of two San Antonio men, who were in a boating accident.
- Glenda Burdick, Rockport Mayor, was honored for her service to the City. MP served as emcee of the event.
- The local Habitat for Humanity dedicated its third home.
- After their boat sank, eight visitors from West Virginia spent the night on an oil platform in Copano Bay.
- Brenda and Ross McElwee's Title IX Complaint was settled. Upon investigation, information indicated no female athletes were treated unfairly.
- Les "Googles" Cole, Fulton Mayor, was honored for his 18 years of service to the Town.
- Mary Casey received the *Jefferson Award Medallion* for her volunteer work with ACMSI.

## MAY

- Forty-three sex offenders were registered in the Rockport-Fulton zip codes.
- Veronica Camehl, ABC Learning Center teacher, had one of her pictures used as the cover photo in *Early Years* magazine.
- The inaugural Rockport Nautical Flea Market was held.
- Mike Womack was elected Mayor of Fulton.

# 30 YEARS THROUGH THE NEWS/LENS

- Todd Pearson was elected Rockport Mayor.
- Jalisco's Restaurant opened at the location of the old Dairy Queen.
- Dabney Hegen was awarded the prestigious *Girl Scout Gold Award*.
- The inaugural life-guarding class was completed at the Community Aquatic Park.
- After a fire was extinguished, Jesse Allen Moore was found dead in his trailer on Lone Star Road. It was later determined he had been stabbed.
- Dylan Conway won the silver medal in discus at the UIL State Track Meet with a throw of 175'1".
- Penny Pinchers opened.

## JUNE

- The Rockport City Council approved on first reading Hogan Homes' Whistler's Cove Subdivision.
- Todd Pearson, Rockport Mayor, proclaimed May 29 as *Vi Street Day*.
- At the RFHS Graduation Ceremony, Floyd Mills received his diploma 59 years late. Because he was called to serve in WWII, he had never received his diploma.
- Samuel John Dillon was killed in a motorcycle accident on Business SH 35 S.
- The Town of Fulton announced it would do its own utility billing.
- Rev. Antonio Vega celebrated his 100th Birthday.
- Construction on the expansion of Business SH 35 came to a halt after the contractor defaulted on the contract.
- Leadership Aransas County Class VI graduated 16, the largest

number to date and the only class to have perfect attendance. *MP was a member of that class.*
- The newsstand price of RP increased to 75 cents.
- The Wendell Family Fireworks Show was set off electronically for the first time.
- The owner of a Fulton Beach Road hotel aired his displeasure about the loud music from area bars.
- Todd Pearson, Rockport Mayor, unveiled *Rockport 20/20*, a vision for Rockport's future, at the RFCC's Annual Banquet.
- Richard Dias was named *Citizen of the Year* at the RFCC's annual banquet.

**JULY**
- HEB opened its new superstore.
- Cody Birk, RFHS track star, received a full scholarship to Oklahoma State University.
- Mike Womack, Fulton Mayor, exposed problems of the Fulton Pier.

The new HEB superstore opened in time for the Fourth of July rush.

# 30 YEARS THROUGH THE NEWS/LENS

- *Lighthouse Fountain*, the newest piece of art in the RCA Sculpture Garden, was dedicated.
- Residents living near the new HEB continued to seek solutions to noise, traffic, and lighting issues.
- MP wrote a column about it being time to end complaints about the new HEB.
- Lewis Robinson, local developer, presented a development concept to the ACND for the Rockport Harborfront.
- Ground was broken on the Lighthouse Inn near Fulton.
- Blue Marlin Car Wash opened.

**AUGUST**

Ground was broken on the Lighthouse Inn. This is the original location of the Paws and Taws.

- South Texas Sports Medicine opened.
- The Fulton Town Council considered forming Fulton's own police department.
- Fish Fest attracted 250-plus parents and kids.
- *The Windswept Oak* was approved as AC's new logo.
- TxDOT held hearings regarding proposed bypass routes from FM 3036 to the Copano Causeway. The crowd was against using Lone Star Road as the highway's footprint.

## 2002: YEAR NINETEEN

- The Rockport City Council approved an ordinance officially making SH 35 bypass a truck route. A "No Trucks" sign was placed at the highway's intersection with FM 3036.
- Susan Combs, State Agriculture Commissioner, visited AC.
- The possible tracking of the water quality of Little Bay was considered.
- Paradise House opened.
- The City of Rockport installed nine new stop signs.
- A fire gutted the former Crystal Daisy Flower Shop.
- Florence Sharp, longtime RP Employee, passed away.

### SEPTEMBER

- Hot Rods & Harleys opened.
- *The South Texas PGA Championship* was played at RCC.

### OCTOBER

- Two cases of West Nile Virus were discovered in AC.
- Hillis Dominguez, longtime ACND commissioner, passed away.
- Buster Gillis, longtime educator and public servant, was killed when a tornado hit a Del Mar College campus in Corpus Christi. Gillis was teaching at that location and was trying to protect students when a wall fell on him. *In the new Live Oak Learning Center, a pirate ship named the SS Buster Gillis, sits in the foyer honoring his many years as principal of Live Oak Elementary.*
- The new terminal building at the AC airport was dedicated and a historical marker was unveiled.

### NOVEMBER

- More than 10 inches of rain fell in some areas of the Coastal Bend. AC received a Federal Disaster Declaration.

# 30 YEARS THROUGH THE NEWS/LENS

The new terminal building is dedicated at the AC Airport.

- Howard Murph defeated Les Cole, Danny Adams defeated Roy Lassiter, and Floyd Clark beat Rudy Nava in contested AC Commissioner elections.
- The ACND dedicated the breakwater at Leggett Light Channel.
- The Band Shell at Rockport Beach Park received a new look.
- The City of Rockport announced water rates were going to increase up to 15 percent.
- RFMS teachers and students conducted a history tour in downtown Rockport.
- *When Angels Weep*, a book about the late Martha Luigi, longtime RHFS choral director, was hot off the press. *This book by Mary Taylor is available for purchase on Amazon.*
- A student committee began working on ideas for a Skate Park with the City of Rockport's Parks Board.

## 2002: YEAR NINETEEN

## DECEMBER

- ❏ The Rockport City Council tabled action regarding Walmart's rezoning request until traffic concerns were answered.
- ❏ A dump truck accident at the corner of FM 3036 and the SH 35 bypass dumped gravel all over the roadway. *In 2013, the driver of that dump truck married MP's youngest daughter.*

# 30 YEARS THROUGH THE NEWS/LENS

## JANUARY

- Melissa Pieper, RFHS senior, received the *Gold Award*, the Girl Scouts' highest award.
- AC Commissioners called a meeting to choose AC Appraisal District Board Members. Glenn Guillory, AC Judge, was not asked to attend. The new court rescinded the decisions made at that meeting.
- The ACND added 20 new boat slips in Rockport Harbor.
- The Fulton Town Council voted down a noise ordinance.
- AC purchased a $40,000 GIS Mapping System.
- Jon House, RFHS head basketball coach, earned his 500th Career Victory.
- Los Comales opened.
- The Fulton Town Council voted down forming a municipal court.

## FEBRUARY

- The Rotary Club honored Patsy Phemister and Janie Ellis for their community service through the RFCC.
- The City of Rockport levied a 180-day moratorium on eight-liners.
- A KKK rally at the AC Courthouse was promoted. Officials urged no attendance. Very few people, other than the news media, attended.
- Dr. Kimberly Maroney opened her practice.

- The RFCC garnered 171 new members during its inaugural *Membership Event*, bringing total membership to 700-plus.
- The Humane Society of AC brought its "No-Kill" request before AC Commissioners.
- The ACND opened new transient shower facilities at Rockport Harbor.
- The design for the new Law Enforcement Center was presented to AC Commissioners. The preliminary plans were rejected. *The Law Enforcement Center and jail are now known as the Public Safety Center and AC Detention Center, respectively.*

## MARCH

- The inaugural Bountiful Bowl Pottery Fair was held.
- The ACISD Education Foundation hosted the inaugural *Shining Stars Over Aransas Banquet.*
- Aransas Bay was considered as a possible site for the proposed National Estuarine Research Reserve, a partnership between NOAA and coastal states. *The Bay Education Center, part of this system, is located at the entrance of Rockport Beach Park.*
- The Holiday Lodge Motel was demolished to make room for the new building at Business SH 35 and Maple Street, which would house Blockbuster Video. *Spanky's Liquor now occupies that location.*
- Buddy McLester, longtime AC constable, passed away.
- The ANWR celebrated a Century of Conservation.
- Coastal Oaks Baptist Church built a new worship center with capacity for 550 people.
- The Town of Fulton formed a Neighborhood Watch Program.

# 30 YEARS THROUGH THE NEWS/LENS

Holiday Lodge Motel was demolished to make room for the building housing Blockbuster Video as its anchor tenant.

The KKK held a rally in March 2003 in front of the AC Courthouse. Only a handful of people attended, but law enforcement's presence was felt.

- ACISD cafeterias switched to point-of-sales systems.

**APRIL**

- Sharkey's Bar was converted into TG's Beachwear.
- MP wrote a column about the need for leadership of local officials with regard to Lewis Robinson's proposed Harborfront Development.

- Skateboard enthusiasts made a presentation to the Rockport City Council about the need for a skate park.
- Mark Gilliam, AC Sheriff, graduated from the FBI Academy.
- Sixteen stop signs were installed in the Oak Terrace Subdivision.
- Members of the RFHS choir, performing at Carnegie Hall in NYC, delivered an American flag made of buttons to NYC firemen. Carolyn Prophet made the flag in the months following 9-11.
- The 4th Annual *Babes on the Bay Fishing Tournament* attracted 108 teams. *The most recent tournament attracted more than 1,300 women.*
- Msgr. Louis Kihneman blessed a statue of the Virgin Mary and Baby Jesus. Phil Ernster ordered the statue from a Vietnamese sculptor and placed it on Fulton Beach Road, near its intersection with Traylor Boulevard. *The statue is now located at St. Peter's Catholic Church on FM 1781.*

## MAY

- More than 350 kayakers participated in *Rockport's Kayak-O-Rama*.
- The sign debate continued in Fulton as another billboard was installed.
- Dylan Conway, RFHS junior, won the gold medal in discus at the 4A UIL State Track Meet.
- The AC Library opened its new children's area.

## JUNE

- A huge fight ensued when Del Mar proposed adding AC to its taxing district through Senate Bill 315. It would have cost local taxpayers $3 million if Gov. Rick Perry signed the

# 30 YEARS THROUGH THE NEWS/LENS

bill. A Political Action Committee was formed. *Gov. Perry eventually vetoed the bill.*

- The City of Rockport incurred a $1 million expense to relocate water lines making way for the expansion of the SH 35 bypass to four lanes.

AC residents let their displeasure be known regarding Del Mar College's attempt to add AC to its taxing district. The governor eventually vetoed the bill after it had passed the House and Senate.

- Justin Muery, RFHS senior, was appointed to the Air Force Academy.
- Fr. Tran Thanh Tung was ordained to the priesthood at Sacred Heart Catholic Church.
- Kam Wagert was named *Citizen of the Year* at the RFCC's annual banquet.
- Adam Watters, RFHS senior, was appointed to the U.S. Naval Academy.
- The required zoning and street closures were approved, making way for the Walmart Supercenter.

**JULY**

- MP wrote a column about his parents' 50th Wedding Anniversary.

## 2003: YEAR TWENTY

- Rev. Tom Wagstaff was named new Vicar at Peace Lutheran Church.
- The infrastructure for La Buena Vida on Business SH 35 S. was being installed.
- Lighthouse Inn opened.
- Funding for the Tri-County Task Force ended, but a grant of $573,394 from the Governor's Criminal Justice Division brought new life to the program.
- The Rockport City Council approved making Water Street a one-way road to allow for a hike and bike lane.
- AC residents braced for Hurricane Claudette's visit, but it made landfall near Port Lavaca.
- An alligator was spotted in Little Bay.
- Habitat for Humanity dedicated its fourth home.
- The demolition of the RPD's old building made room for the new Public Safety Center.
- A viewing scope was dedicated at the Connie Hagar Wildlife Sanctuary on Little Bay near McDonalds.
- TMM announced that LaSalle Odyssey's first exhibit would open, one of five permanent exhibits.

The RPD station was torn down to make room for the Public Safety Center.

# 30 YEARS THROUGH THE NEWS/LENS

- The Rockport Yacht Club opened its expanded facilities on Rockport Harbor.

## AUGUST

- MP wrote a column about his parent's first cruise experience.
- Backpacks were prohibited at RFMS.
- The Council on Government reported AC was the fastest growing county in the Coastal Bend at a rate of 29.6 percent.
- The City of Rockport unveiled its new logo.
- Dana Taggart published *Open His Gift*, a book containing answers to many of life's questions.
- A new scoreboard was installed at Pirate stadium.
- The ACISD made an attempt to bring a Naval Junior Reserve Officers Training Corps (JROTC) to the district.

LaSalle's Odyssey exhibit at the TMM opened with much fanfare.

## 2003: YEAR TWENTY

The new scoreboard at Pirate Stadium, as well as the new concession stand, background, was in place before the start of the 2003 football season.

## SEPTEMBER

- The City of Rockport was selected as a *Target Community* for a study conducted by Texas A&M for Landscape Architecture and Urban Planning Departments.
- Coldwell Banker–The Ron Brown Co. opened.
- A groundbreaking was held for the new Public Safety Center at 714 E. Concho Street.
- Richard Richard won $1,000 in RP's Power Points of the Southwest Football Contest.

Ground was broken in September 2003 on the new Public Safety Center, across the street from Sacred Heart Catholic Church.

# 30 YEARS THROUGH THE NEWS/LENS

- The Rockport City Council approved a resolution encouraging redevelopment of vacant buildings east of the City's downtown business district.
- Don Douglass rescued the lone survivor of a boating accident. The victims were from Mississippi.
- Sigwald Service Co. received the *Better Business Bureau of the Coastal Bend Torch Award*.
- MacPort Dry Stack Storage was under construction at Cove Harbor. More than 500 boats can be stored there.
- Pazera Capital Management opened.
- Charlie Porter battled the vibrio virus.
- A second rezoning request for property on Tule Drive, across from Companion Animal Clinic, failed.

## OCTOBER

- Construction crews made the foundation footprint for the AC Detention Center and Public Safety Center.
- Property values in AC increased 94 percent in 20 years.
- Oak Crest Nursing Center broke ground on a 20-bed secured unit for Alzheimer's patients.
- Capt. John Muery retired from the TPWD after 31 years.
- Walmart's Tree Plan was approved.
- A workshop was held to discuss the future of downtown Rockport.

## NOVEMBER

- The AC Reclamation District's funding ended with the assignment of its water contract to the City of Rockport.
- Concho Street, in front of the AC Detention Center, was closed to through traffic.

## 2003: YEAR TWENTY

- Twenty-one Date and Washingtonia palms, relocated from the old Hunt's Courts on S. Austin Street, were planted at Rockport Beach Park.
- The City of Rockport brought utility billing in-house.
- The ACND tabled action regarding the reassignment of the $312 Surf Court Motel lease, which was later reassigned through 2009.
- Plans for the $13 million Camp Aranzazu were unveiled.
- Todd Pearson, Rockport Mayor, and Martha, his wife, were featured on the cover of a popular magazine.
- The Texas School Counselors Association named Gail Roaten, *Counselor of the Year.*

Rockport's Mayor, Todd Pearson, and his wife, Martha, were featured on the cover of *Where to Retire* magazine.

- Paula Bell was named Fulton Postmaster.
- Rockport Birding and Kayak Adventures opened.
- About 500 people attended a reception and book signing for the *Texas Most Wanted*, Sporting & Wildlife Art Exhibit at the RCA.

# 30 YEARS THROUGH THE NEWS/LENS

- ❏ The Rockport Beach Nourishment Project was underway.
- ❏ A Dallas man, caught with a dead Whooping Crane, faced jail time and a large fine.
- ❏ A sign at Veterans Park to honor local military personnel was approved by the ACND.

**DECEMBER**

- ❏ The RFCC kicked off its *Fall In Love with Rockport-Fulton* advertising campaign.
- ❏ MP wrote a column about his oldest daughter getting her drivers license.
- ❏ Lewis Robinson outlined his Rockport Harborfront project with his first proposed Memorandum of Understanding.

## JANUARY

- A 1,000-acre brush fire, which began off Janecek Road, kept firefighters up all night.
- The Simmons family mourned the death of 17-month-old Baija, who passed away in Ohio due to blunt force trauma to the abdomen.
- David's Supermarket located at Harbor Oaks Village Shopping Center closed.
- The City of Rockport's Public Works Department moved into its new 4,480-square-foot facility on Laurel Street. The building cost less than $175,000.
- Eight-liners were seized at a Fulton business.
- The Biennial Quilt Show was held. *The event began as a beach event by the Piecemakers Quilt Club and the RFCC in an effort to create a beach activity per month. Quilts continue to be displayed biennially at the RFHS Commons.*
- An ACSO Deputy shot a suspicious man twice in front of Casterline Seafood.
- AC Commissioners approved a tax freeze for property owners 65 and over as well as for those who are disabled.
- City of Rockport staff was directed to investigate creating a Tax Increment Reinvestment Zone for the proposed Rockport Harborfront project.

## FEBRUARY

- Lewis Robinson removed all plans for his Rockport Harborfront Development.

# 30 YEARS THROUGH THE NEWS/LENS

- ❑ The RFCC kicked off its *Fall In Love with Rockport-Fulton* advertising campaign at RCC by making a toast to Rockport and Fulton.
- ❑ Aransas First, whose mission is the identification, restoration, and preservation of the sensitive wildlife habitat in AC, put out a plea to purchase 30 acres along Tule Creek between the new Walmart and old Walmart, for a proposed green belt.
- ❑ TxDOT projects in AC topped $35 million.
- ❑ Two dead landmark live oak trees at SeaAire Shopping Center were removed.

The two landmark live oak trees at SeaAire Shopping Center were removed during construction of Business SH 35.

- ❑ MP wrote a column about how much the community had changed during his first 20 years in Rockport-Fulton.
- ❑ The ACND proposed to revitalize the boat ramp at Cove Harbor with funds from a TPWD grant.
- ❑ Gary Smith was honored for 50 years of service to the RVFD.

## 2004: YEAR TWENTY ONE

- The Rockport Beach Renourishment Project, including the planting of salt-tolerant vegetation along the new dune line, was completed.

## MARCH

- Ken Schrupp, owner of Best Western in Fulton, alleged misuse of the Town of Fulton's HOT money.
- An ACISD Appreciation Dinner was held at the 25th annual Oysterfest and was a huge success.
- Cady Bryant, a student in Bobby Jackson's history class at RFMS, wrote about his desire to "bring back" the big blue crab. *A new blue crab graces the waterfront at the south end of the Rockport ski basin.*
- Wayne Johnson, ACISD Superintendent, announced because ACISD was labeled as a Chapter 41 district, $1.3 million of local school tax money would have to be sent back to the State and then sent to "poor" districts.
- Curvy character palms were planted at Triangle Park and Rockport Beach Park. *Triangle Park, located in the green space between Broadway, Sabinal and Patton, is now named Compass Rose Park.*
- Carr's Cleaners & Laundry opened.
- Linda Burgess, former Town Secretary of Fulton, was given vacation pay, but was denied severance pay by the Town Council.
- The ACND asked the City of Rockport to drop the requirement to pay the City $25,000 annually if the Rockport Beach Park operated at a net loss. *The Rockport Beach Park always operated at a loss.*
- MP wrote a column about his family's first trip to New York City.

# 30 YEARS THROUGH THE NEWS/LENS

- Construction on the new Walmart Supercenter changed the skyline.
- Compton Docks removed a storage tank, which had become an eyesore, on SH 35 N. in Fulton, near FM 1781.
- Ken Schrupp headed the *Clean Sweep Committee*, a catalyst for change, in Fulton.
- Stewart Title Co. gave the RFCC a new marquee sign to be used at the RFCC to announce events.

**APRIL**

- William Adams, AC Court-At-Law Judge, reported his department was paying its own way.
- A fire destroyed a home on Blue Heron Circle in Key Allegro with weather cited as a probable cause.
- Shelly Kay was hired as the RFHS varsity girls' basketball coach.
- The Whooping Crane Strut attracted more than 100 participants. *The Strut is in its 26th year.*

The trees in this photo, taken during construction on Business SH 35, make it look as though there is a hill behind SeaAire Shopping Center.

## 2004: YEAR TWENTY ONE

- Dylan Conway, RFHS track standout, signed a letter of intent to attend Texas A&M University College Station on an athletic scholarship.
- Jean Berry, ACISD Secretary to the Superintendent, retired after 20 years of service.
- The ACISD brought the sister of a Columbine shooting victim to speak to fifth through 12th grade students.
- The ACND set a policy ending live bait sales from boats.
- The Coastal Bend Pony League held opening ceremonies for its inaugural season.
- Kay McMahan's recipe for "Tomato Tart" was selected for publication in *American Profile*.
- Billy Pash, a suspended ACISD bus driver, shot two ACISD employees after an altercation.

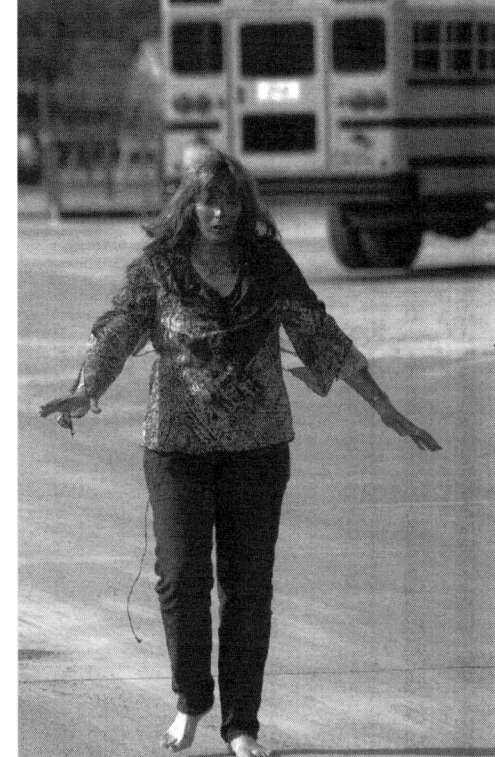

A suspended ACISD bus driver shot two ACISD employees, including this woman who ran toward authorities at the scene.

### MAY

- The Rockport City Council began new discussions about a long-term solution to the problematic entrance to Key Allegro.

# 30 YEARS THROUGH THE NEWS/LENS

- Asa Yeamans was appointed to the State Windstorm Code Committee.
- Moon Dog's Seaside Eatery opened. *This restaurant was recently renovated and additional seating was added.*
- Farmers/Burns Insurance opened.
- Fulton paid AC its three-year debt for law enforcement services.
- RP received the *Community Service Award* given by the Texas Gulf Coast Press Association for the newspaper's effort to kill the Del Mar College Tax Bill.
- Dylan Conway won the silver medal in discus in his third trip to the state track meet.
- Black skimmers chose to nest on the beach instead of nesting in the site prepared for them.
- Nancy Arispe defeated Russel Cole in the Fulton Mayoral Race.
- Phil Barnes was hired as the Curator at the TMM.
- Karen Pieper, RFHS student, was first in the nation in *Business Professionals of America Word Processing Competition. Pieper also placed nationally in 2005.*
- David Lowell, RFHS senior, was honored for never missing a day of school from kindergarten thru 12th grade.
- Laura Denham, Candy Schreck and MP sang, *I'm a Man of Constant Sorrow* at the RFCC's Business Showcase
- A new Fulton Town Council was sworn in, the *Clean Sweep Campaign* elected Nancy Arispe Mayor, as well as Larry Pearce and Gary Cooper, Aldermen. Outgoing mayor Alene Mundine, who was appointed mayor after Mike Womack died in office, turned the chair over to Arispe saying, "I turn my chair over to you with all its problems."

- H.R. Bean recounted his experiences at Pearl Harbor and during World War II.
- Bill Christian, founder of the TMM, was honored at the Festival of Wines with a *Lifetime Achievement Award*.

## JUNE

- Mark Uhr proposed a townhome development next to the Paws and Taws called Poinciana Bay. *The proposed site remains undeveloped.*
- The RFHS Software Pirate team made up of Bill Hamilton, Patrick Harrington and Klaus Zanders, along with John Owen, Computer Science Teacher, placed first in a national contest in Chicago.
- A cellphone tower was proposed between Palmetto and Broadway streets, east of 3rd Street. Questions regarding safety during a hurricane eventually led to changing the site to the old Fulton Rodeo Grounds.
- Gateway Computers donated eight laptop computers to be used by ACISD Trustees.
- The portraits of Ronald Yeager and Alonzo Rodriguez, retired District Judges, were hung in the district courtroom.
- Thom Evans was named 2004 Art Festival Poster Artist.
- The Rockport City Council denied Boy Scout Troop 49 and Ship 49 sailboat usage in the ski basin due to hazardous conditions with motorized watercraft.
- Two structure fires, in the 1800 block of Business SH 35 and in the 200 block of Cornwall Street, started within 30 minutes of each other.
- New banners were placed on the downtown Rockport light standards.
- MP wrote a column about the death of President Ronald Reagan.

# 30 YEARS THROUGH THE NEWS/LENS

- The RFCC held its inaugural *Youth Leadership Conference* with 27 RFHS students participating.
- MP wrote a column about his body not being what it was in college, after planting more than 20 pallets of grass in his new yard.
- The TMM opened its remodeled Museum Store.
- More than 50 animals were removed from a home on FM 1781; 19 of them were euthanized after being found in deplorable conditions.
- Marisa Rinche traveled to Hawaii to play in a USA Volleyball Tournament.

## JULY

- The TMM celebrated its 15th Anniversary with the christening/rededication of the *Texas Scow Sloop*.
- AC Commissioners approved funding $2,000 to assist with the hydraulic analysis of Cedar Bayou.
- Bellino's Italian Restaurant opened.
- Castaways gave the ACEMS $25,000 to assist in the purchase of a new mobile intensive care unit.
- Tom Staley was named *Citizen of the Year* at the RFCC's annual banquet.
- The Fulton Town Council was split in a 3 to 3 vote with regard to paying the ACSO for law enforcement services.
- Gov. Rick Perry appointed Mark Gilliam, AC Sheriff, to the State Jail Commission.
- Construction began on the ACISD's new technology building on the north side of Pirate Stadium.
- The Rockport City Council approved Richard Ehrlich, concessionaire, to locate his self-contained trailer at the Rockport

Beach Park. *Ehrlich continues to sell shaved ice treats from that trailer.*

## AUGUST

- A bomb threat, called in from a stolen cell phone, kept local law enforcement authorities on their toes. Later the threat was determined to be a hoax.
- The Fulton Town Council approved creating a municipal court. C.M. Henkel agreed to take the job for one year at no salary.
- AC Commissioners threatened to cut back ACSO coverage in Fulton if the town refused to pay for services.
- Gov. Rick Perry appointed Glenn Guillory, AC Judge, as Chairman of the Region Review Committee of the Coastal Bend COG.
- Ed Hegen of the TPWD Coastal Fisheries Division said the aquarium could be reinstated in approximately 18 months.
- Dos Dietze, former Rockport resident, was arrested after a double shooting at the intersection of FM 1069 and the SH 35 bypass; both men were transported to area hospitals.
- Waterfront parking was restricted at Rockport Harbor due to the weakened integrity of the steel tie-ins attached to the bulkhead.
- James "Red Dog" Ashley survived in Copano Bay for almost nine hours after falling off his sailboat in rough waters. He found and held on to Crab Trap Float No. 199 until Marty Martin, TPWD Game Warden, rescued him.
- San Jacinto Title opened.
- The Public Safety Center opened.

# 30 YEARS THROUGH THE NEWS/LENS

City of Rockport and Aransas County elected officials cut the ribbon opening the Public Safety Center.

## SEPTEMBER

- A fire destroyed a detached building at Sportsman Manor Hotel, which was used as a laundry room.
- ACE Hardware opened in Harbor Oaks Village Shopping Center.
- Point-of-sale Vehicle Registration was implemented at the AC Tax Assessor-Collector's office.
- Jessica Pham, student at Fulton Learning Center, had her artwork chosen for the ANWR Billboard.
- The driver of an RV swerved to miss an ice chest in the road, turned over, and landed on top of an SUV on the SH 35 bypass. It took three hours to free the three victims, who all survived.
- Mitch Ammons, RVFD Chief, said all trees near a roadway needed to be trimmed to a 12'2" clearance to make room for the RVFD's new aerial ladder truck.
- The RFCC added *Sea-A-Bration* to Seafair. *Proceeds from the kickoff party are now used to pay off the debt on the RFCC's new offices and Visitor's Center.*

## 2004: YEAR TWENTY ONE

- A large donation by Ceil Frost opened the door for upgrades to the Martha Luigi Auditorium.
- MP wrote a column about a car accident occurring in front of his house, which involved his oldest daughter and two of her close friends.
- The Rockport-Fulton A&M Club was formed with John Debler serving as its first President.
- The ACND learned major bulkhead repairs were needed at Rockport Harbor. Boat owners were notified stern-in docking was prohibited.

**OCTOBER**

- *Travel 50 and Beyond* magazine named Rockport one of 10 great retirement towns.
- Ron Blue, local craftsman/artisan, restored a historic boat built by Barney Farley, FDR's Port Aransas fishing guide.
- A local group set a goal to have 50 care packages ready to send to troops in Iraq.

A crowd was waiting to shop when the ribbon was finally cut opening the new Walmart Supercenter.

# 30 YEARS THROUGH THE NEWS/LENS

- Walmart Supercenter opened.
- The Fulton Town Council considered publishing a newsletter to be mailed to all residents.

**NOVEMBER**

- An open house was held to share information about Young Life and what the organization could do for our community.
- AC Commissioners negotiated housing federal inmates. Up to $789,000 could be realized in additional revenue by opening up a third pod at the AC Detention Center.
- Sam Spears opened his Edward Jones office.
- Ground was broken for the Hampton Inn.
- Rio Grande Valley Birding Festival named the HummerBird Celebration, one of the *Earliest and Best Birding Festivals*.
- The RVFD paid cash for its new $624,000 aerial fire truck.

**DECEMBER**

The Wells Fargo Town Hall was the last such bank facility to be demolished.

## 2004: YEAR TWENTY ONE

It was magical when it snowed almost five inches on Christmas Eve 2004!

- The Wells Fargo Town Hall was demolished.
- Edward J. McNelis, owner of Texas Directory Co., Inc. of Rockport, was selected as *2004 Ronald Reagan Republican Gold Medal Award Winner* for Outstanding Business and Leadership.
- Burton Owens III, 32, was arrested after admitting to committing 21 burglaries of businesses in downtown Rockport.
- On Christmas Eve, it snowed approximately five inches in AC for the first time in more than 100 years.

# 30 YEARS THROUGH THE NEWS/LENS

## JANUARY

- A $24 transferable parking permit was introduced at the Rockport Beach Park.
- Steve Russell, local and internationally-known artist, published his book, *Notes by Texas Painter. A Russell painting sold for more than $14,000 at the 2014 Rockport Art Festival auction.*
- Karen Pieper, Kellie Green, Heather Jack, Tyson Ruhmann, and Alexis Saski, RFHS choir members, were named to the UIL All-State Choir.
- Record crowds turned out for the 10th Annual Rockport Gospel Festival.
- Agnes A. "Tony" Harden, 77, former AC Judge and County Clerk, passed away.
- U.S. Marine Corps officials notified the family of Matthew Holloway that he had been killed in Iraq.
- The City of Rockport made plans for a major drainage ditch near the Whistler's Cove Subdivision.
- The Del Camino Motel on Business SH 35 was demolished. *It was replaced by Poor Man's Country Club Restaurant & Bar.*

## FEBRUARY

- A quarter of Rockport voters approved a permanent tax freeze 929 to 388 votes for those over 65 and those with disabilities.
- The developers of Olde Town Place planted palm trees, which changed the face of the land across from the ski basin.

- Dallas Franklin and Kelcey Cruser, RFHS swimmers, advanced to the UIL State Swim Meet.
- North Bay Hospital filed for Chapter 11 bankruptcy noting $20 million in debts.
- The City of Rockport planted 40 trees at the Wastewater Treatment Plant on Arbor Day.
- Nancy Melcher was named Queen of the TMM's *10th Annual Mahjong Tournament*.
- The RFCC membership neared 1,000 with 275 new members gained during the Membership Event.
- Kelcey Cruser, RFHS senior, was appointed to the United States Naval Academy.
- MP wrote a column about his Grandma celebrating her 100th birthday.

## MARCH
- Concrete barriers were placed between the AC Courthouse and the AC Detention Center to eliminate through traffic.
- MP wrote a column outlining reasons the ACEMS needed to find a new funding source.
- Rain forced the early end to the 26th Annual Fulton Oysterfest.
- The Fulton Town Council discussed forming a Planning and Zoning Commission.
- Wayne Johnson, ACISD Superintendent, implemented the chant, "Whatever It Takes," in all his talks.
- A bill that would have added AC taxpayers to the Del Mar College Taxing District was revived. HB 2221, filed by State Rep. Vilma Luna, D-Corpus Christi, began the second round of debates about the issue.

# 30 YEARS THROUGH THE NEWS/LENS

- The local office of the Texas Department of Human Services faced closure.
- A human skull and bones were found on Johnson Road by construction workers.
- Sixteen vehicular accidents were reported in AC during Spring Break.
- MP wrote a column in support of the formation of the Heritage District in Rockport.
- A tree was dedicated in memory of Matthew Holloway, soldier killed in Iraq, at RFHS across from the Martha Luigi Auditorium.
- Houston's Lakeland Development made plans to buy 12 acres from the Bass Family and work through five leases with the ACND in order to develop the Rockport Harborfront. *Those plans never materialized.*
- Carl Krueger, 77, local community leader and developer of Key Allegro, passed away.
- The national average price for a gallon of regular unleaded gas was $2.15.
- Latitude 28'02 expanded and opened a full service bar.

## APRIL

- Cecil Arnett, RFHS golf coach, died the day after his team advanced to the Regional Tournament.
- The ACND received a $250,000 TPWD grant for improvements to the boat ramp at Cove Harbor North.
- A threat to a teacher caused a two-hour lock down at ACISD campuses.
- The offices for AC Treasurer and Auditor were moved to their new space, which had formerly been the ACSO.

## 2005: YEAR TWENTY TWO

- Dawn Whidden, RFHS Lady Pirate varsity soccer coach, was named *Coach of the Year*.
- The Rockport City Council approved placing antennas on top of one of the City's water towers in lieu of allowing the construction of a cell tower.
- The City of Rockport approved a 25-year lease with Aransas First for that organization's preservation of habitat and wildlife in AC.
- The Texas A&M Press donated 50 books to the AC library in memory of Carl Krueger.
- Local Aggies held their first Aggie Muster as a club.

The Rockport-Fulton A&M Club held its first Muster as a club with R.C. Slocum, third from left, giving the keynote speech.

- The City of Rockport bought an AM frequency for $22,715 to use during emergencies or to broadcast tourist information and community events.

# 30 YEARS THROUGH THE NEWS/LENS

- E.J. Mendoza, Justin Longoria, Matt Benavides and Ben Setterbo, members of the RFHS 800-meter and mile relay teams, along with Ryan McMakin, who threw the shot put, represented the ACISD at the state track meet. McMakin won the bronze medal.

**MAY**

- Karen Pieper, RFHS senior, was awarded Girl Scout's highest honor, the *Gold Award*.
- Bahia Bay residents put together care packages for U.S. Troops.
- The National Interscholastic Swimming Coaches of America named Kelcey Cruser, RFHS swimmer, *Academic All-American*.
- MP wrote a column about making it through his daughter's first senior prom.
- Shop the World opened.
- MP wrote a column about the non-prosecution of certain DWIs.
- Walmart named Susan Beree, *Teacher of the Year*.
- Great Clips opened.
- Rockport Downtown Merchants held its inaugural Heritage Day.

**JUNE**

- American Bank opened.
- The nesting site for black skimmers at the Rockport Beach Park was changed to the area of the circle drive.
- MP wrote a column about his father reaching his 50th Anniversary as a Lutheran Pastor.
- William Barr and Stuart Burleson were hired as ACISD athletic director and head football coach, respectively.

- The Annual Wendell family fireworks display was dedicated to the memory of Carl Krueger.
- The RFCC earned 4-star Accreditation from the U.S. Chamber of Commerce.
- Work began on Goose Island Marsh Restoration and Shoreline Stabilization.
- Aggregate sales tax revenues were up 18.97 percent through the first half of the year.

## JULY

- When the awning of Loung's Restaurant, formerly Corky's Restaurant, was removed, the old sign for Rockport Electric Co. was uncovered.
- A employee from Corpus Christi was fatally injured in an elevator accident at Degussa on Business SH 35 S. *Degussa is no longer in business. All buildings have been removed.*
- Traci McLester, former RFHS athlete, school officials and parents gathered for the presentation of a $5,000 award from Coca-Cola. *The money was used to buy a new score board in the Gold Gym at RFHS.*
- Rockport Skate Park opened next to the pool at the Community Aquatic Park.
- The 100 Club of AC donated bicycles to the RPD.
- China Bay Restaurant opened in the former Burger King building. *It is currently Panda Bay restaurant.*
- Mary Lucille Jackson, RCA Executive Director, resigned. She was getting married and moving to England.
- A second hospital proposal for AC was made. *No hospital has been located in AC.*

# 30 YEARS THROUGH THE NEWS/LENS

**AUGUST**
- Rick McLester, ACSO Chief Deputy, received the *Texas Peacemaker Award*.
- At the RFCC luncheon, the ACND's $23 million Waterfront Bond Issue was explained.
- RP published a series of five articles about the ACND Bond Issue.
- The Fulton Town Council approved a Farmer's Market at Fulton Harbor.
- The TMM received accreditation from the American Association of Museums.

**SEPTEMBER**
- Austin Street Gallery opened.

AC residents banded together to collect and deliver aid for Hurricane Katrina victims.

## 2005: YEAR TWENTY TWO

- *Diane Probst Day* was proclaimed in recognition of her 15 years of service at the RFCC.
- AC Commissioners opened Airport Park behind the AC Airport on FM 1781. *It was later renamed Howard Murph Park in honor of the late AC commissioner, who led the effort to create the park.*
- The old AC Jail was demolished.

The old AC jail was demolished in September 2005.

- AC voters overwhelmingly defeated the ACND Bond Issue.
- A trip to NYC attended by City of Rockport officials led to a better bond rating and $150,000 in savings in interest on the City's debt.
- Nicole Gloor was hired as the ACISD Education Foundation's first full time Executive Director.
- Bill Christian, 81, the father of Seafair, the TMM, and Coast Watchers, passed away.

# 30 YEARS THROUGH THE NEWS/LENS

## OCTOBER

- A foundation was formed to establish and operate a technical college in AC.
- Kelli Green, RFHS student, was a National Merit Scholarship Semifinalist.
- Bobby Jackson, RFMS Texas History Teacher, was named *Education Service Center's Region 2 Secondary Teacher of the Year.*
- Local game wardens traveled to New Orleans to lend a helping hand after Hurricane Katrina.
- RFHS hosted the inaugural Coastal Bend Marching Festival with up to 15 bands participating. *The festival is no longer held.*
- The RVFD bought a thermal imaging camera.
- Seafair was dedicated to the late Bill Christian.
- Rules for Redfish Bay Seagrass Protection were proposed to prevent propeller scarring of the grasses.
- The ACND took control of Copano Bay pier operations.
- The 100,000th guest entered the Community Aquatic Park.
- Todd Adams and Tommy Ramzinsky won the *Walmart FLW Redfish Series Championship* along with its $75,000 prize.
- Beverly Morgan was named RCA Executive Director.
- Caitlin Arambula, RFHS track star, advanced to her second consecutive UIL State Cross-Country Meet.

## NOVEMBER

- The old office at Key Allegro Marina was moved via barge to Cove Harbor to make room for a condominium development called Marina Club.

- The City of Rockport installed dune crossovers at the Rockport Beach Park.
- The Marina Association of Texas presented John and Larie Nelson, owners of Key Allegro Marina, *The 2005 Marina of the Year Award.*
- Bishop Edmund Carmody attended the reopening of Stella Maris Chapel.
- Bracht Lumber Co. was sold to Park Lumber. *It is now known as Pro Build.*
- Buildings were demolished to make room for Starbucks. *Burger King is now located in the old Starbucks building.*

**DECEMBER**

- Margaret Sue Rust, local philanthropist, passed away.
- Fortress Storage opened.
- Supporters of Nancy Arispe, Fulton Mayor, condemned the actions of the Town Council, which took away her mayoral powers.
- A new aquarium was considered at the TPWD on Rockport Harbor.

# 30 YEARS THROUGH THE NEWS/LENS

## JANUARY

- Herman Johnson, Rockport's first City Manager, passed away.
- State Rep. Glenn Hegar of Katy sought the Texas Senate Seat, which serves AC. *He was elected, and in 2014 sought the position of Texas State Comptroller.*
- The City of Rockport's new logo was placed on the sign at City Hall.
- Dat Nguyen's fans packed into the Big D RV Park and Pat's Place for a book signing for his new book *Dat: Tackling Life and the NFL*.
- Ground was broken on the 280-acre Iron Gator Development on the SH 35 bypass at the AC and San Patricio County lines. *It is now called Southern Oaks Luxury RV Park and has yet to be fully developed.*

RFHS, Texas A&M, and Dallas Cowboy gridiron star Dat Nguyen signs copies of his new book at Pat's Place.

## 2006: YEAR TWENTY THREE

## FEBRUARY

- *Relish*, a monthly food magazine, was added to RP.
- The ACND announced 48 new boat slips would be built at Rockport Harbor.
- A focus group, including Bass Family representatives, studied height restrictions for future harborfront developments.
- The Fulton Town Council chose not to annex six Live Oak tracts.
- Kathryn Childers, local TV celebrity, presented a $10,000 check from proceeds of her book, *Snow*, to Aransas First.
- Castaways gave $50,000 to the ACEMS to purchase two new ambulances.
- MP wrote a column about meeting John Wooden, legendary UCLA basketball coach.
- A couple visiting from out of town were killed in a local motel in an apparent murder/suicide.
- The bridge leading into Key Allegro was renamed *The Carl C. Krueger Jr. Memorial Bridge*.
- AC Commissioners approved a 10 percent match for a $3.3 million Airport Improvement Grant.

The *America's Most Wanted* TV show focused on the 2001 murder of the Hunt's Castle owner investigated by RPD's Larry Sinclair.

# 30 YEARS THROUGH THE NEWS/LENS

- Elected officials and officials from the ACEMS, RVFD, and FVFD met with an expert regarding the formation of an Emergency Services District, a permanent way to fund those organizations.
- The *America's Most Wanted* TV show focused on the unsolved 2001 murder of the owner of Hunt's Castle.

## MARCH

- Work began on a secondary exit from Copano Cove to give residents a second outlet to FM 1781.
- Hampton Inn received a five-foot variance for its sign.
- Gary Cooper, Fulton Alderman, died after suffering a major stroke.
- Michael Heil, 13-year-old pianist, placed at the *National Finals* in Austin.
- Holy Cross Lutheran Church broke ground on its new church on FM 3036.
- The Rockport Heritage District joined forces with Master Gardeners to plant native plants in 50 barrels along Austin Street in downtown Rockport.

## APRIL

- The Rockport City Council approved *A Vision for the Heritage District and Downtown Rockport*, a comprehensive master plan.
- The speed limit on the SH 35 bypass inside the city limits of Rockport was lowered from 70 to 60 mph.
- The viewing shelter/kiosk was dedicated at end of the boardwalk at Cove Harbor Wildlife Sanctuary.
- The inaugural *Relay for Life* at Pirate Stadium raised almost $80K for the local American Cancer Society.

## 2006: YEAR TWENTY THREE

- The ACND stopped public access to the Rockport Harbor Breakwater to ease further deterioration.
- Duke Eaton, former Major League Baseball Umpire, threw out the first pitch at the opening ceremonies for the Rockport-Fulton Little League.
- Tami Noling was awarded the Grander Marlin Trophy after being named the *WBS World Champion of Bill Fishing*, the first woman to win that title.
- Volunteers from First United Methodist Church loaded a trailer and headed to Waveland, MS to help Hurricane Katrina victims.
- Russel Cole, Fulton Alderman, took a stand at a Fulton Town Council Meeting regarding the removal of Nancy Arispe, Mayor.
- AC Commissioners approved the purchase of Reverse 911.
- C.H. "Burt" Mills defeated Danny Adams by 46 votes in the GOP Primary Runoff Election.
- Giggles Ice Cream Bar opened.
- Coastal Bend Adult Day Care opened.
- The City of Rockport approved the submission of an application for a proposed new visitor's center, to house the RFCC, ACND, and NERR on ACND property near the entrance to the Rockport Beach Park.
- The offices of Key Allegro Real Estate were expanded by 1,400 square feet.
- In an open letter to residents, Nancy Arispe, Fulton Mayor, responded to Russel Cole's charges.
- Amazing 20/20 Window Cleaning opened.
- A new boating law aimed at protecting seagrass went into effect.

# 30 YEARS THROUGH THE NEWS/LENS

The creation of the Mission-Aransas NERR became official at a ceremony in Port Aransas, which included U.S. Senator Kay Bailey Hutchison, and University of Texas President William Powers.

## MAY

- Work began on a major drainage project off FM 2165 designed to address drainage issues in that area.
- Elaine Faulkner, a 10-year TMM employee, was surprised with a day named in her honor when she retired.
- The Mission-Aransas National Estuarine Research Reserve became official.
- Those elected in Fulton's earlier *Clean Sweep* Election were swept out of office. Russel Cole was elected Mayor, while Carol Thompson and Dale Owens were elected Aldermen.
- Justin Longoria won the silver medal in the 400-meter dash at the UIL State Track Meet, setting new school and personal records with a time of 48.05 seconds. *The world record time for this event is 43.18 seconds held by Michael Johnson.*
- MP wrote a column under the headline "Okay Fulton, What Direction Now?"

## 2006: YEAR TWENTY THREE

- MP wrote a column under the headline "Where did the time go?" about his oldest daughter graduating from high school.
- Lulu's Flowers opened.
- Ryan McMakin and Shannon Cunningham, RFHS track athletes, signed letters of intent with UTSA and Angelo State, respectively.

## JUNE

- Christus Spohn purchased property at the southwest corner of FM 2165 and the SH 35 bypass and planned an August groundbreaking for an Urgent Care Center. *Those plans never materialized.*
- MP wrote a column about the death of Perry Bass, the owner of St. Joseph's Island, the Fort Worth philanthropist who loved AC, and whose family owns St. Joseph's Island..
- AC Commissioners set aside $100,000 in HOT funds for the RFCC's proposed Visitor's Center.
- Margaux Development Co., the owner of the old HEB in downtown Rockport, talked to Rockport Heritage District Association representatives about development of the property.
- Hampton Inn and Suites opened.
- Justin Longoria received a partial scholarship to run track at Texas State University.
- A groundbreaking was held for Paradise Bay Condos at 1401 S. Fulton Beach Road. *That project never came to fruition.*
- First Victoria National Bank broke ground on its new facility at the corner of Business SH 35 and Enterprise Boulevard. *Joe Meyers Exxon was demolished to make way for the new bank.*

# 30 YEARS THROUGH THE NEWS/LENS

- A portion of Nancy Ann Street was permanently closed to make room for the Fulton Mansion's new Education and Visitor Center.

**JULY**

- Eight inches of rain fell in two hours flooding many areas of AC.

Eight inches of rain in two hours overwhelmed the City of Rockport's storm drainage system, causing flooding in areas which usually don't flood.

- Camp Aranzazu opened its doors to its first camper. *The first phase of the camp is located off FM 1781 at the former site of the Bishop Elliot Conference Center.*
- The old cabanas on the waterfront next to the RCA were demolished and replaced with new ones.
- Bobby Jackson was named *Citizen of the Year* at the RFCC's annual banquet.
- The Rockport School received historic designation via a historical marker.

## 2006: YEAR TWENTY THREE

- Lamar Pointe Preserve, located on SH 35 near Lamar, was opened for property sales. *The development of this property was originally begun in the mid-80s.*
- TxDOT turned over ownership of a portion of Loop 70 (Austin Street in downtown Rockport) to the City of Rockport.
- A new DVD was developed by the RFCC to promote AC.

## AUGUST

- The new Chaparral Street Lift Station in Fulton was under construction. The nearly $1 million project included 14,000 linear feet of sewer line to connect with the City of Rockport's sanitary sewer system.
- The ACEMS promoted the use of blue reflective address signs for homes and businesses to aid in locating those seeking emergency treatment.
- AC Commissioners approved giving Charlie's Place, a drug and alcohol recovery center in Corpus Christi, $35,000. Talks began regarding setting up a similar facility in AC.
- AC Commissioners gave Aransas First $45,000 from the County's HOT funds to be used for an engineering study for Tule Lake restoration.
- Brett Phillips and Mike Patterson won the top prize of $40,000 in the *O Boy! Oberto Redfish Cup in Port Aransas.*
- The ACND approved a grant for a restroom/shower facility at Fulton Harbor.
- The ACND increased festival ground rental fees to $50 per day.

## SEPTEMBER

- Construction on a new Speedy Stop was underway at the corner of FM 3036 and SH 35.

# 30 YEARS THROUGH THE NEWS/LENS

- AC Commissioners voted 4-1 to add the fourth pod to the AC Detention Center.
- Alexis Saski blew away the competition with her performance at the MGM Grand in Las Vegas against 700 contestants. She was named *Top Overall Performer* and *Top Female Vocalist. Saski continues to live in Rockport and Nashville, TN and is noted for being a Christian, Gospel, Pop, and Rock singer/ songwriter.*
- The price of a gallon of regular unleaded gas was $2.09.
- Tony Tellez drowned when the horse he was riding ran into a pond.
- Daniel Carpenter, James and Missy Beck, and Pat Smolik were recognized for heroism by Todd Pearson, Rockport Mayor, for saving the life of Harlee Hartman, 11, when she got caught in a storm drain after 12 inches of rain fell in AC.
- The City of Rockport released the free parking area of the Rockport Beach Park to the ACND.
- The West Nile Virus was detected in local mosquitoes.
- Fulton voters approved funding bonds to be used for street, drainage, and sewer projects.

**OCTOBER**

- The Sanctuary at Camp Aranzazu was dedicated. It was a gift from John Watson to Prissy, his wife.
- Pat and George Hall were crowned *Sea Queen* and *Sea King* in recognition for their work with Seafair.
- MP wrote a column about back pain after spending the weekend moving his oldest daughter into her first college dorm.
- C-Side Decorating opened.

## NOVEMBER

- The Rockport Heritage District signs were installed in downtown Rockport.
- The bond issue to fund $6 million in Rockport Harbor Improvements was approved by voters.
- Juan Garcia defeated Gene Seaman in the race for AC's state representative. *Geanie Morrison now holds that position.*
- C.H. "Burt" Mills was elected AC Judge.
- Stuart Burleson, RFHS head football coach, said he was fired.
- John Owen earned the rank of Eagle Scout.

## DECEMBER

- Glenn Guillory, retiring AC Judge, was recognized during a special reception.
- The City of Rockport put a new twist on its Christmas celebration by using fireworks to close the Rockport Tropical Christmas Celebration.
- AC Commissioners approved funding $30,400 for an aquarium at the TPWD maintenance building at Rockport Harbor.
- Main Street Arts opened. *The First Baptist Church was located there before it moved to its new building located at the intersection of Live Oak Street and Enterprise Boulevard.*

Rockport Heritage District signs in downtown Rockport were installed in three locations.

# 30 YEARS THROUGH THE NEWS/LENS

- Ground was broken on Sea Oaks Village, a subdivision between FM 3036 and Chaparral Street in Fulton.
- Caitlin Arambula, RFHS senior cross-country runner, signed a letter of intent to attend Texas A&M-Corpus Christi.
- First Victoria Bank opened at the corner of Enterprise Boulevard and Business SH 35. *First Victoria Bank sold to Prosperity Bank and ceased operations in Rockport. 1st Community Bank is now located there.*
- The ACND approved the construction of a second dry stack storage facility at Cove Harbor.

## JANUARY

❏ Local Circle K Convenience Stores were converted to Stripes.

❏ A four-way stop was installed at the intersection of Live Oak and Orleans Streets.

❏ Preliminary design guidelines for the Heritage District were revealed.

❏ The Technical College Foundation donated $10,000 to the ACISD Education Foundation to fund scholarships for students, who met specific criteria in the technical trades.

❏ Guy Grover, the former Bandera football coach, was hired as RFHS' new head football coach and boys' athletic coordinator.

Circle K convenience stores were converted to Stripes.

❏ An agreement between the City of Rockport and Town of Fulton, swapping land in each entity's extraterritorial jurisdiction, ended all future growth by Fulton in terms of

# 30 YEARS THROUGH THE NEWS/LENS

- additional acreage. Fulton was completely surrounded by land controlled by Rockport.
- Sea turtle bones, more than 100 years old, were found during test digging for the Fulton Mansion's new Visitors Center.
- A camera was placed on the TMM's Lighthouse making it a "WeatherBug Weather Station".

**FEBRUARY**

- Ricky Lee Pady was found guilty in the July 2004 murder of Denise Elizabeth Ortman and was sentenced to 50 years in prison.
- Cell phones were banned on ACISD campuses during TAKS testing.
- MP wrote a column calling for the Rockport City Council to make changes in the height restrictions in strictly regulated Planned Unit Developments.
- The inaugural Coastal Bend Travel Fair drew a crowd of 400 to the Paws and Taws Convention Center.
- A troubled son killed his parents in their Lamar home, shot at Will Newsom, ACSO deputy, and then killed himself.
- MP wrote a column about his grandmother dying before she reached her 102nd birthday.
- Dat Nguyen was hired as the Dallas Cowboys' assistant coach.
- The $3.4 million TxDOT project widening FM 1781, from SH 35 to FM 1069, was underway.
- The ACND approved a temporary site for the new aquarium.
- Texas Tech University began microfilming old copies of RP.
- Vie's Ocean Nails & Spa opened.

RFMS Texas History Teacher Bobby Jackson led the Historic Walking Tour in downtown Rockport.

- A replica of *La Nina*, one of the reproduced Columbus ships, sailed to Rockport and was open for tours.
- Holy Cross Lutheran Church was dedicated.
- Bobby Jackson led the Historic Walking Tour of downtown Rockport.

**MARCH**

- The ACISD Education Foundation announced its $1 million Endowment Fund Drive.
- A new law allowed for the cancellation of elections in non-contested races.
- The Moore House on S. Church Street was issued its historical marker.
- Ron Roe, ACND Harbormaster/Superintendent, died suddenly after suffering a heart attack.

# 30 YEARS THROUGH THE NEWS/LENS

- The TMM unveiled its *Sports Fishing Wall of Fame*, named in honor of Perry R. Bass.
- The Rockport City Council, on a 3-2 vote, approved a new height restriction of 74-feet in a Planned Unit Development (PUD) in the Heritage District.
- Five individuals donated more than $20,000 to support equipping a RPD Tactical Unit.

**APRIL**

- *Keep Rockport Beautiful* called for all dumpsters to be hidden and locked.
- A new 30-foot octagonal, open air, mini-pavilion was announced for the end of the Rockport Beach Park.
- The Coastal Bend Pony League kicked off its season naming *Otis Field* and *Augie Field* after Mike Otis and Augie Garcia, respectively.
- A $100,000 donation from the Margaret Sue Rust Foundation kicked off the capital campaign to build a new ACEMS building.
- A pilot landed his plane in Copano Bay and swam to shore.
- MP wrote a column about his youngest daughter being accepted to Texas A&M.
- Joseph Patek was hired as ACISD Associate Superintendent.
- A gazebo near the community pool and skate park was

A pilot crashed his plane into Copano Bay and swam to shore.

dedicated in honor of Glenda Burdick, former Rockport Mayor.
- Rick Roe was posthumously honored with the *2006 OSPRA Award*.

## MAY
- Humpal Physical Therapy opened.
- The TMM received approval to build a vault for receivership of curatorial and educational items.
- Rockport Marine opened.
- The Fulton Town Council approved a big sewer rate hike.
- Betty and Curtis Dunn of Fulton won a new car on *The Price Is Right*.
- Talks began with City of Rockport officials for the development of the Oaks at Bentwater apartments.
- The AC Ministerial Alliance united to provide the first Community Table at the Presbyterian Church. *The Community Table continues to serve meals every Tuesday beginning at 4:40 p.m.*
- Randall Rickerson of Corpus Christi caught the state record bull shark in local waters. It weighed 513 pounds and was nine feet long. The previous state record was 508 pounds.

## JUNE
- The Police Chief from Waveland, MS talked about the devastation of Hurricane Katrina. He said coming here was scary because Rockport-Fulton looked a lot like Waveland before the storm.
- MP wrote a column focusing on the need for a new building for ACEMS and called for additional donations.
- Volunteers painted the inside of the TPWD Maintenance Building to make the Aquarium at Rockport Harbor operational.

# 30 YEARS THROUGH THE NEWS/LENS

- Sushi Luck Restaurant made a proposal to the Fulton Town Council to open a Japanese Restaurant. The council turned down the request. *The owners then located the restaurant one street to the south on Palmetto Street in Rockport.*
- Proposals by Margaux Development for the old HEB site, including the closure of one block of Austin Street, required rezoning and public hearings.
- Allied Waste Services proposed starting a new automated collection service. *That service never materialized.*
- Keith Barrett was hired as ACND Harbormaster.
- The Patriot Guard Riders welcomed home Maj. John Blackwell after a 12-month tour in Iraq.
- MP wrote a column stating there was no practical, long-term reason for keeping the block of Austin Street, next to the old HEB, open to traffic.
- Storm sewer pipes were installed along Linden and Live Oak Streets to complete a major storm sewer upgrade in the City of Rockport.
- The bleachers at Pirate Stadium received new aluminum seats and walkways.
- Wayne Johnson, ACISD Superintendent, was named *Education Service Center, Region 2, Superintendent of the Year.*
- The Rockport City Council approved a Planned Unit Development (PUD) for the old HEB and the closure of one block of Austin Street, next to the old HEB. *The development never materialized. The RFCC eventually moved into the former Rockport City Hall across the street from the old HEB and Austin Street remains open.*
- Houston's Lakeland Development Company proposed a $75 million redevelopment of the legendary Sea Gun in Lamar.

## 2007: YEAR TWENTY FOUR

## JULY

- The ACND approved experimental seagrass planting in Little Bay.
- The RPD formed a Special Response Team (SRT).
- A motorist destroyed eight planters in downtown Rockport.
- Rockport Websites opened.
- Bad weather forced the groundbreaking of a Chili's Restaurant indoors. *K-Bob's Steakhouse is now in that location.*
- Maison Et Jardin opened.
- Larry Crabb's story, about seeing an image of his deceased brother in a photo, aired on the Montel Williams show.
- Ground was broken on the ACEMS' new 12,000-square-foot facility.
- MP wrote a column about buying new bikes after his youngest daughter left for college.
- Jack Wright was named *Citizen of the Year* at the RFCC's annual banquet.
- The Rockport Area Association of Realtors (RAAR) moved to its new home on Traylor Avenue, behind IBC Bank.
- The Aquarium at Rockport Harbor opened next to the TPWD. *Admission continues to be free.*

## AUGUST

- Dr. Bob Mayberry suddenly passed away at 52, leaving many people without a physician.
- Bloomer's Nursery opened.
- Karl Fisher earned the rank of Eagle Scout.
- AC and City of Rockport officials broke ground on a new animal shelter on Airport Road.

# 30 YEARS THROUGH THE NEWS/LENS

- ACISD trustees called for a $40 million bond election to renovate Live Oak Learning Center and Fulton Learning Center, as well as purchase school buses.

**SEPTEMBER**

- Sgt. Garrett McLeod, RFHS graduate, was killed in a helicopter crash in Iraq. Hundreds brought him home.
- Duck Inn Restaurant closed its doors after 60 years in business.
- The ACND questioned the City of Rockport's downtown drainage plans. Eventually, the plans were approved and the project completed.
- The Royal Oaks Development opened.
- The ACSO received a donation from Chris and Karra Crowley to purchase a Canine Unit. The money was used to purchase Deputy Flaco, who was used to search school property for drugs.

When the body of Sgt. Garrett McLeod, RFHS graduate, was brought home, hundreds lined the highway leading to the funeral home.

# 2007: YEAR TWENTY FOUR

The iconic Duck Inn closed its doors for the final time in 2007.

## OCTOBER

- The local Habitat for Humanity dedicated its sixth home.
- RP switched to a narrower web width, but the length of the newspaper remained unchanged.
- Capt. Benny's Seafood & Oyster Bar opened.
- Jim Anderson, AC Attorney, announced he would not seek reelection after eight terms in office.
- The inaugural Rockport Film Festival was announced by the RCA.

## NOVEMBER

- The Birding Observation Deck at Rockport Beach Park received a makeover, including a new lattice roof.
- The ACISD's $40 million Bond Issue failed.
- Four ACND incumbents were ousted. The remaining commissioner in office was in an uncontested race.
- The latest count showed there was a record 241 Whooping Cranes wintering in and around the ANWR. *As of 2013, 78 mating pairs and a total of 279 birds were counted.*

# 30 YEARS THROUGH THE NEWS/LENS

The building next to the old Whataburger had to be moved to make room for the new Whataburger.

- The Fulton Town Council approved a noise ordinance setting the maximum level to 70 decibels, 24 hours a day, seven days a week.
- The building directly north of the old Whataburger was moved to make room for a new Whataburger.
- Todd Pearson, Rockport Mayor, was elected president of the Texas Municipal League.
- Spanish Woods residents complained about speeding motorists and requested speed bumps be installed.

**DECEMBER**

- Virginia Shivers, 97, AC's only lady sheriff, passed away.
- Fulton's Annual Winter Texan Fish Fry drew a crowd of more than 1,000 people.
- The new boat ramp and restrooms at Cove Harbor were opened.
- Martha McLeod, Fulton Learning Center Teacher, was recognized as *Texas Teacher of the Year* at a ceremony in Austin.
- Local artist Kay Barnebey's Christmas ornament "Cycle of

## 2007: YEAR TWENTY FOUR

Life," representative of the Life Cycle of the Kemp's Ridley Sea Turtle, was selected as one of the ornaments to be hung on the White House Christmas tree. The ornament became a permanent art piece to be kept at the White House. Kay traveled to Washington, D.C. to see her ornament hanging on the tree in the Blue Room with others representing the other U.S. National Parks.

- The effort to bring back the Big Blue Crab took a new direction with the *Bring Back The Big Blue Crab Fundraising Effort*.
- Dr. Kyle Mason and Dr. Ron Ramey, local dentists, merged their operations at a new location.
- State officials helped dedicate a new Bilge Water Facility at Cove Harbor.
- Oscar Pina, AC Commissioner, announced he would not seek reelection to the office he had held for almost five terms.
- John Ryan Johnson was sentenced to 15 years in prison on child pornography charges.
- Ground was broken on the Live Oak Medical Clinic on FM 3036.

# 30 YEARS THROUGH THE NEWS/LENS

## JANUARY

- Philip Baldwin, Chester Barre, Katie Lee Clarke, Buster Gillis and Dave Segler were selected as the first *ACISD Wall of Honor* honorees.
- The ACEMS received a $250,000 donation from the Sid Richardson Foundation and a $500,000 donation from Ceil Frost, in memory of her daughter, to bring the amount raised for the new ACEMS building to $1.1 million.
- Walter Knight, 53, former pastor of First Baptist Church, suddenly passed away.
- The bulkhead repair project at Rockport Harbor was underway.
- Rockport School was designated a historic landmark. *Built in 1953, the building served as an educational and a community institution. As a school, grades one through eleven were taught here.*

Rockport School was designated a historic landmark in January 2008.

## FEBRUARY

- Diane Probst, President/CEO of the RFCC, was named *Chairman of Texas Chamber of Commerce Executives*.
- Lola L. Bonner, pioneer for AC women and attorney, passed away.
- MP wrote a column about the possible "brain drain" the City of Rockport could suffer with pending retirements of long-tenured employees.
- Dairy Queen expanded, adding a 50-seat private dining room and 50 new parking spaces.
- Steven Gould, author of *Jumper*, attended the opening of the movie of the same name at Cinema 4.
- Joseph Patek was named ACISD Superintendent.
- Panels for the breakwater in Rockport Harbor were installed.

## MARCH

- Bill Mills unseated Mark Gilliam, incumbent AC Sheriff, in the Republican Primary election.
- Two homes in the 1200 block of Water Street were destroyed by fire.
- AC received an $800,000 Rural Community Affairs Grant for sewer improvements in the Smith and Wood Subdivision.
- Vi Street, a well-known local volunteer, passed away.
- The death of an 18-month-old child was declared a homicide.

## APRIL

- Members of the AC Clean Team were recognized for their efforts, which resulted in the Parade of Palms Project.
- Ground was broken for the new sign at the entrance to the ACND Festival Grounds, a class project of the Leadership Aransas County Class XII.

# 30 YEARS THROUGH THE NEWS/LENS

- The City of Rockport purchased the Aransas Natural Gas Company.
- A sculpture of *Kemp's Ridley Turtle* was added to the RCA Sculpture Garden with funds provided by members of the Thomas Moore family.
- ACISD trustees approved the construction of eight new tennis courts at a cost of $500,000.
- The ACND helped obtain an Aquarist on staff for the Aquarium at Rockport Harbor.
- Bay Breeze Animal Clinic opened.
- The RFHS Band won the *UIL Sweepstakes Award* at UIL Region Band Concert and Sight Reading Competition.
- The AC Animal Control Shelter opened.

## MAY

- Steve Fischer beat incumbent Rusty Little in the ACISD Trustee Election.
- Todd Pearson was reelected Rockport mayor for his final term due to the City's 10-year term limits.
- A local Great Texas Birding Classic *Big Sit Team* sighted 68 species in one sitting.
- The new ACEMS Facility opened.
- Virginia Tanner was killed in a late night fire on Moline Street.
- Rebecca Moriarty (then Lee) was named *2008 Babe of the Year* at the Babes on the Bay Fishing Tournament.
- A Texas Capital Fund Grant helped pay for improvements to sidewalks and street paving on Austin Street in downtown Rockport.
- Darryl Black, a local fisherman, caught a record crevalle jack in Port Bay.

## 2008: YEAR TWENTY FIVE

The ACEMS facility provided much-needed space in which to operate.

- Arthur Cantu State Farm Insurance opened.
- The 50th Anniversary of the *1958 Beach Tragedy* was remembered. Seven people drowned that day trying to save a person, who had slipped into a deep hole.
- Heritage Day, celebrated with old-fashioned events and special awards, marked the City of Rockport's 137th Anniversary.
- Oh My! opened.
- Fifty-three dachshunds were seized in an animal cruelty case.

**JUNE**

- The RFHS Class of 2008 boasted 175 students.
- Plans were unveiled for the Reserve at St. Charles Bay, a Hal Jones development.
- A crash on the Copano Causeway killed Herman Dabbs, 81. He was in the wrong place at the wrong time as someone tried to pass him.

# 30 YEARS THROUGH THE NEWS/LENS

- Brad Frome, a 17-year RP employee, died after a lengthy illness.
- The historic Sea Gun structure was leveled.
- The AC Stormwater Advisory Committee was established.
- Upgrades to restroom and shower facilities at Goose Island State Park were completed.
- Stella Maris Chapel celebrated its 150th year Anniversary.
- A $4.4 million project to rehabilitate 13 miles of streets in the City of Rockport was underway.
- After being elected AC Commissioner, Jack Chaney, ACISD Trustee, resigned from the school board.
- Camp Aranzazu dedicated its 8,000-square-foot open-air concrete covered pavilion.

The historic Sea Gun structure was leveled in June 2008

## 2008: YEAR TWENTY FIVE

## JULY

- A $125,000 facelift for Pirate Stadium provided better drainage, a sprinkler system, reset the crown on the field, and added new grass.
- Boat ramp renovations at Cove Harbor South were completed.
- James H. Sorenson, Jr., longtime Rockport banker, community leader, philanthropist, and mentor to many, passed away eight days short of his 90 birthday.
- A new pavilion, horseshoe pits, and a dog waste station were installed at Fulton Navigation Park.
- The City of Rockport investigated possible solutions to a growing roof rat problem.
- Juliet Wenger, pioneer journalist and broadcaster, passed away.
- A fire at 11 Curlew on Key Allegro destroyed a home and yacht.

## AUGUST

- Susie Bracht Black was named *Citizen of the Year* at the RFCC's annual banquet.
- Jesus Moroles and Suzanna, his sister, were honored guests of President George W. Bush and First Lady Laura Bush at a Cinco De Mayo Celebration Dinner in the White House Rose Garden.
- The ACISD was the only 4A or 5A School District in Region 2 to earn a "Recognized" status from the Texas Education Agency.
- U.S. Senator Kay Bailey Hutchison spoke at the TMM's 20th Anniversary Celebration.
- The Rockport City Council approved installing a three-way

stop sign at the intersection of Bayshore and Mazatlan drives on Key Allegro.
- The Rockport City Council denied the rezoning request of Holiday Inn Express to build a four-story hotel on Lady Claire Street.
- The old Whataburger closed its doors so that a new restaurant could be built next door. The new restaurant was slated to be open by Thanksgiving.
- MP wrote a column about his Alaskan cruise with his extended family. While in college, he had driven to Alaska on a vacation 29 years earlier.
- The Blue Lagoon Water Park was proposed at a site on the SH 35 bypass. *The water park was never built.*

## SEPTEMBER
- Randy White, Dallas Cowboy Hall of Famer, visited Rockport.
- Huey Rey Fischer received an appointment as Senate Page by U.S. Senator Kay Bailey Hutchison.
- Tisha Piwetz, RFHS Principal, was named *Texas Association of Secondary School Principals Principal of the Year*.
- Hurricane Ike eyed the Texas coast and local officials discussed evacuation procedures. When Ike made landfall in Galveston, AC became the site of an unplanned "Hurri-cation," or an evacuation from a major hurricane, which turns into a short holiday.

## OCTOBER
- The Texas Historical Commission acquired two lots from the City of Rockport to make way for the construction of the Fulton Mansion's new Education and History Center.
- Pat Daly, Precinct 2 Justice of the Peace, was honored in the district courtroom on his 80th Birthday.

## 2008: YEAR TWENTY FIVE

- AC commissioners proclaimed *Carla Reed Day* in recognition of her work sending care packages to troops overseas.
- AC Commissioners tabled action regarding joining the Regional Corpus Christi Economic Development Corporation, which had requested a $25,000 contribution. *The court later gave the group $10,000.*
- A local bird bander captured a ruby-throated hummingbird, which had previously been banded in North Carolina.
- Mark Gilliam, AC Sheriff, resigned. AC Commissioners appointed Bill Mills, Sheriff-Elect, to the post.

New bulbouts at intersections in downtown Rockport changed motorists' driving habits.

- The RCA Sculpture Garden received a new piece of art given by Cam Leonard. Sculptor Jesus Moroles unveiled the piece called *Umlauf's Uccelli*.

### NOVEMBER
- Rockport Young Life celebrated its 10th Birthday.

# 30 YEARS THROUGH THE NEWS/LENS

- TxDOT officials presented Copano Causeway alternatives during a public meeting on the campus of Little Bay Primary. Ironically, a crash closed the causeway for a brief period of time five days after the hearing.
- President George W. Bush presented Jesus Moroles, the *2008 National Medal of Arts*, in a ceremony in the East Room of the White House.
- The City of Rockport was selected for the *Visionaries in Preservation Program*, which included a planning grant to develop a strategy for the Historic Preservation in AC.
- Diana Kirby left her post at the Fulton Mansion to assume a promotion as Historic Sites Supervisor. Dr. Marsha Hendrix was named new Manager of the Mansion.

**DECEMBER**

- Martin DeLeon, Precinct 1 justice of the peace, resigned.
- Oscar Pina, retiring AC Commissioner, and Jim Anderson, retiring AC Attorney, were recognized at a reception for their lengthy terms of service.
- The new Whataburger opened.
- Guy Grover was promoted to ACISD athletic director and head football coach.
- The resurfacing project at the ACND Festival Grounds began.
- The City of Rockport approved the purchase of 36 acres. *The property would remain in its natural state to improve the drainage system of Tule Creek. It also provided space for another segment of the City's Hike and Bike Trail System.*
- John Woods, RFHS graduate, received a full scholarship to play football at Lamar University.
- The ACMSI's *Little Old Ladies in Tennis Shoes* hung up their tennis shoes, leaving behind a legacy of fundraising for the ACMSI.

## 2008: YEAR TWENTY FIVE

- Gary Howard, RPD commander of criminal investigations, retired after a 25-year career in law enforcement.
- Jamie Wagner Sengvanhpheng, 21, an RFHS graduate, drowned after driving his car off the Copano Causeway Pier.
- Tackle Town burglars escaped with $50,000 worth of merchandise.

# 30 YEARS THROUGH THE NEWS/LENS

## JANUARY

- Degussa announced it was closing down its Carbon Black Plant on Business SH 35 between Rockport and Aransas Pass.
- The RFCC Visitor Center reported a record 200th Visitor in one day.
- The new ACISD tennis complex opened.
- Travis Wright shot and killed his friend, Leonard Minns, 29, on his doorstep.
- Penny Neff received the *Shield of Sparta Award*.
- Dennis R. King Sr. was hired as the City of Rockport's new Public Works Director. Billy Dick was promoted to Director of Utilities, a new position.

The ACISD cut the ribbon on its new Tennis Complex.

- AC Commissioners said they would negotiate a contract with Naismith Engineering for the AC Stormwater Plan.
- Mack Forty Dog Kennel opened.
- The *Rockport in Bloom Contest* was announced.

**FEBRUARY**
- Sudoku made its debut in RP.
- Oaks at Bentwater Apartments opened.
- Approximately 100 volunteers from 15 fire departments battled a brush fire that burned 160 acres. As a result, the SH 35 bypass was closed for a short time.
- MP wrote a column about the body and mind not always being in sync after reflecting about playing in a benefit basketball game.
- The Swenchonis family sought justice in the death of their son, who was killed in the terrorists' 2000 bombing of the USS Cole. The father sends a letter annually to Yemen's President.
- Salt Flats Photography opened.

While playing in a benefit basketball tournament against the Harlem Ambassadors, MP thought he could still play ball like he did in college.

# 30 YEARS THROUGH THE NEWS/LENS

- Diane Dupnik was chosen as Precinct 1 Justice of the Peace from eight applicants.
- The Margaret Sue Rust Foundation donated $25,000 to the Odyssey After School Program.

**MARCH**

- Marco & Co. acquired Outside the Box Weddings and Parties.
- The 30th Annual Fulton Oysterfest drew huge crowds.
- The Texas Historical Commission told AC Commissioners the AC Courthouse was an example of 1950s architecture and must be preserved.
- Sarah Gomez of Aransas Pass was hit twice by two different vehicles and killed, while walking in the southbound lane of the SH 35 bypass shortly after midnight.
- A sketch by Shirley Blackman of the City of Rockport's Downtown Master Plan began to take shape.
- Marine Cpl. E4 Cody Collins returned home.
- Scott McLeod, TPWD Game warden, was named *Game Warden of the Year*, and Karen Meador, a Natural Resource Specialist, was named *Biologist of the Year*.
- The RFMS Band won the Sweepstakes Award at UIL Band Competition.
- The City of Rockport purchased 20 acres from Al Johnson to add to Memorial Park.
- The inaugural *Women in the Wild Event* was planned for April.
- The endangered Whooping Crane had a difficult year, suffering the highest mortality rate in 20 years. *The Whooping Cranes numbered 270 in 2008, but fell to 247 in 2009.*
- The RFCC requested AC Commissioners form a Venue Tax Task Force for development of a venue on festival grounds.

## APRIL

- AC Commissioners hired Naismith Engineering to develop the Countywide Drainage Plan at a cost of $290,600.
- John Owen, RFHS educator, received the *Lifetime Achievement Award* from HEB for Excellence in Education.
- Shawn Kilpatrick, Will Douglas, Betsy Farmer, and Connor Lyon were named to the UIL All-State Choir.
- Historic preservation goals were prioritized during a session of the *Visionaries in Preservation Program*.
- AC Commissioners examined their options regarding the AC Courthouse.
- Construction on the TMM's Maritime Collections and Education Center was well underway.
- Paradise Key Island Grill located at the Key Allegro Marina was the site of 100 citizens attending a local version of the Tea Party Project, which were being held across the nation.
- The City of Rockport sought requests for proposals to design a multipurpose community center to be located next to the Community Aquatic

More than 100 residents gathered for a local version of the Tea Party Project.

# 30 YEARS THROUGH THE NEWS/LENS

The Compass Rose Labyrinth was officially opened with a ribbon cutting.

and Skate Park. *The facility was never built.*

- AC Commissioners approved spending $94,000 in HOT Funds to repair the roof for the Aquarium at Rockport Harbor and for the return of the airshow. *Commissioner Howard Murph tried to assemble a committee for the airshow, but it never materialized.*
- The Compass Rose Labyrinth at Triangle Park, across from the ski basin, was dedicated. *The park is now named Compass Rose Park.*
- AC Commissioners hired a consultant to study possible uses of the Degussa Property. The plant had been shut down since January.
- The ACND officially opened its new boat ramp at the south end of the Copano Bay Causeway.
- The RFCC gained 213 new members during its Membership Event.
- A Swine Flu outbreak caused UIL schedule changes in schools.

## MAY

- Kevin Lynch, RFHS senior, signed a letter of intent to play basketball at Schreiner University. *He later transferred to Texas A&M Corpus Christi.*
- The Roadrunner Youth Birding Team won first place in the *Great Texas Birding Classic.*
- AC property owners let their voices be heard in Austin regarding Windstorm Insurance Rates.
- A boating accident in Copano Bay caused four people to swim to shore. One of the victims drowned.
- Laura Adams was named *2009 Babe of the Year* at the Babes on the Bay Fishing Tournament.
- The Margaret Sue Rust Foundation gave $30,600 in support of MAXA, the Math and Computer Science Academy at RFHS.
- Funds from the Sudan were freed for *USS Cole* Families. Gary and Debbie Swenchonis fought for seven years for justice in their son's death.

An AC delegation met with other Coastal Bend officials in Austin to speak out against Windstorm Insurance rates.

# 30 YEARS THROUGH THE NEWS/LENS

The Fulton Town Council selected the location of the Little Sign Shop for a new parking lot in downtown Fulton.

## JUNE

- A four-way stop was installed at the intersection of the SH 35 bypass and FM 1069.
- The location of The Little Sign Shop was selected to build a parking lot by the Town of Fulton.
- The community room at the AC Library received a facelift.
- The Galveston Chamber of Commerce shared Hurricane Ike recovery secrets with the RFCC staff.
- Herb Wisch, Rockport councilman, died in his sleep.
- Lisa Baer, local resident and business owner, was named Poster Artist for the 40th Annual Rockport Art Festival.
- C-Side Decorating was the first local business to receive a revised Small Business Administration 7(a) Loan.
- The Free Card Program was implemented at the AC Transfer Station.
- GIGNAC Architects were awarded the design contract to

## 2009: YEAR TWENTY SIX

build the Mission Aransas NERR's Bay Education Center. That facility is located on ACND property near the entrance to Rockport Beach Park.

### JULY

- AC Commissioners approved the purchase of a fire hydrant for Holiday Beach.
- The north *Welcome* sign was refurbished and a new wood barrier wall was added.
- The Daily Grind Coffee Shop opened.
- Texas First Lady Anita Perry provided the keynote address at the TMM's 20th Anniversary Celebration.
- Ceil Frost was recognized during *An Eight Year Late Plaque Ceremony*. She did not like being recognized, but Mary Taylor coordinated the ceremony. The plaque is located at the entrance to the community pool.
- Orvis opened.
- The Fulton Town Council swapped a 250' x 250' section of the old rodeo grounds for the property owned by the FVFD. This deal paved the way for the new FVFD fire station.
- A seven-foot granite sculpture named *Days* was moved from Austin Street in downtown Rockport to the RCA.
- MTV TV Show, *Tr3s*, auditions were held at the Saltwater Pavilion.
- David Beckham and Tiny, his wife, restored the historic Train Depot on Magnolia Street.
- The RVFD received approval to improve its Henderson Street Fire Station, adding a 1,050-square-foot steel building.
- MP wrote a column reflecting on the passing of Johnnie Vermillion. *MP lived in Vermillion's home for a short time when he moved to Rockport in 1984.*

# 30 YEARS THROUGH THE NEWS/LENS

- Jerry Nash, a popular RFHS teacher and coach, was found dead in his home.
- Barbara Long was named *Citizen of the Year* at the RFCC's Annual Banquet.
- Aranda's Mexican Grill opened.
- The Rockport City Council froze the medical benefits of retired City employees.

**AUGUST**

- The ACISD received a Texas Education Agency "Recognized" rating for the second consecutive year.
- John Jackson, founder of the ACISD Education Foundation, was honored and received a commemorative RFHS football.
- AC Commissioners approved a resolution to begin the process of purchasing the entire block east of the courthouse, which is planned as the site for a new courthouse sometime in the future.
- Cary Clawson painted a mural on the RFHS Gym floor.
- A report showed AC had a 6.1 percent increase in tourism spending from 2007 to 2008. A total of $97.2 million was recorded as direct travel spending in AC.
- Susie Bracht Black offered her cookbook, *Recipes and Remembrances*, during a book signing at IBC Bank.
- JD's Cove Harbor Cafe opened.
- The City of Rockport installed four speed humps on Spanish Woods Drive in a pilot project.

**SEPTEMBER**

- First Impressions House Staging opened.
- Congressman Ron Paul addressed a crowd at a Town Hall Meeting at the Saltwater Pavilion.

## 2009: YEAR TWENTY SIX

- A hand grenade was found in a box of donated items at Castaways. The Corpus Christi Bomb Squad was called in to detonate the device.
- The Rockport City Council refinanced the City's bonds, saving taxpayers $221,713. An additional $10.3 million in Certificates of Obligation for Capital Projects was approved.
- Gerald Shedd, ACND Commissioner, turned in his letter of resignation, then changed his mind before the ACND board could approve it.
- Lloyd "Midnight" Longoria, a pedestrian, who crossed Business SH 35 near Market Street after dark, was struck by Constable Mike Gregg. Longoria later died from his injuries.
- Rockport Donuts opened.
- Dale Owens, Fulton Alderman, resigned.
- An AC mosquito truck ran into Sears in Fulton releasing its mosquito spray inside the building. *The store remained closed until the lethal spray was cleared and damage repaired.*
- Mike Patterson and Brett Phillips, Rockport Fishing Guides, won the *2009 IFA Redfish Tour Event* held in Port Aransas, and won a boat valued at $30,000.
- The RFHS and RFMS Band Programs received national honors in the *2009 National Wind Band Project Competition*.
- Texas Children's Hospital received a $1 million donation in memory of Lee Ellis, son of Rockport's Janie and Jim Ellis.
- Dr. Terry Colley, Texas Historical Commission Deputy Executive Director, presented copies of the completed VIP Action Plan. All entities presented proclamations.

**OCTOBER**
- Marvine Wix, AC treasurer, retired after 27 years of service.
- Cell phone use in school zones was made illegal.

# 30 YEARS THROUGH THE NEWS/LENS

- The AC Road and Bridge Crew cleaned the debris from Tule Lake, behind the old Walmart.
- A marble slab weighing 1,000 pounds fell off the east side of the AC Courthouse during the night.
- The Fulton Town Council approved a $1.4 million bid to improve the infrastructure of downtown Fulton.

**NOVEMBER**

- MP wrote a column about finally getting to go on a swamp tour in Louisiana on his 50th Birthday. *MP was born in New Orleans.*
- Construction on the new Holiday Inn Express was underway.
- The City of Rockport hired a Public Information Spokesperson.
- Developers of the Islands of Rockport announced that the Corps of Engineers had approved their permit.
- MP wrote a column stating the City of Rockport's decision to join the City of Alpine's lawsuit regarding open meetings was a bad idea. *The courts eventually ruled against the City.*
- Beau Kelly earned the rank of Eagle Scout.
- Brandi Huff, RFHS senior, signed a letter of intent to play basketball at Texas A&M Corpus Christi.
- *Off Port Bow*, a sculpture, was unveiled at the RCA in honor of Lola L. Bonner, local attorney.
- Tom Ward opened the doors to a vacation home for Wounded Warriors, to be used as a getaway for veterans and their families.
- The Aransas Project sought proper management of Guadalupe River Basin Water Outflows to local bays.
- MP wrote a column about his oldest daughter receiving her Aggie ring in a ceremony, which was much grander than when he received his in 1980.

## 2009: YEAR TWENTY SIX

- AC Commissioners approved hiring PFK Consulting for a Conference Center Feasibility Survey.

**DECEMBER**

- The Lamar VFD began receiving utility surcharge funds, which will raise about $3,600 annually.
- Rex Hoyt invented a fishing lure called *The Rockport Rattler*.
- The Rockport City Council approved Rockport Market Days.
- The AC Woman's Club Building received a historical marker.
- Kent Riley and West, his grandson, were killed in a plane crash near Bergstrom Airport in Austin. Riley was instrumental in the formation of Young Life in Rockport-Fulton.
- Tammie Shelton was appointed Camp Aranzazu's Executive Director.
- The Tule Hike and Bike Trail was carved out of the wooded area near Walmart.
- Sassy opened.
- The Rockport City Council said it wanted the pool partners to share the community pool's deficit.
- Plans for the Aquarium Education Center's addition were approved by the ACND.
- The Daughters of the Republic of Texas presented MP with a flag that had flown over the Alamo.
- Janie Ellis won the *Texas Coastal Bend Regional Tourism Council's Award for Tourism Excellence* for her work at the RFCC.
- The City of Rockport was one of four cities joining an Open Meetings Lawsuit filed in Federal Court.

# 30 YEARS THROUGH THE NEWS/LENS

## JANUARY

- Judy Nibbelink, the granddaughter of Rockport's first newspaper publisher, Charles Francis Bailey, reflected on the past. *Bailey Pavilion, which once jutted into Aransas Bay, was a popular gathering place.*
- Two Whooping Cranes made their way to a field off Eighth Street in Lamar and attracted a steady stream of birders lining the roadways for a quick look.
- The results of the Conference Center Feasibility Study said any facility needed to be on the water to be competitive in the market, and should not exceed 18,000 square feet.
- James Fox, Danny Adams Sr. and the late Howard Brown were inducted into the *Perry R. Bass Memorial Sports Fishing Wall of Fame at the TMM.*

## FEBRUARY

- RFHS dropped down from 4A Classification to 3A.
- Aransas First dedicated the Tule Creek Nature Center at Tule Creek Marsh East.
- The Texas Attorney General said the four cities involved in the Open Meetings Lawsuit had to withdraw.
- Jeremy Solis earned the rank of Eagle Scout.
- Chili's Grill & Bar closed its doors. *K-Bob's is currently located there.*
- The City of Rockport's Parks Maintenance Staff moved into a new facility on the west side of Memorial Park.

- The RPD sought new law enforcement equipment with funds from a $1.3 million Homeland Security Grant.
- Camp Aranzazu welcomed Bum Phillips, former Houston Oilers Coach, to the organization's Board of Directors.

## MARCH

- Meetings about the City of Rockport's Sanitary Sewer Discharge Permit drew large crowds.
- Shellie Caballero was crowned *Miss Oysterfest* in the inaugural Miss Oysterfest Scholarship Pageant.
- Pete Chamberlain received the *Mason's Community Builder Award*.
- Aransas Project filed a Federal Lawsuit to protect the habitat of the Whooping Cranes.
- The City of Rockport sent a notice of violation to the ACND regarding trash and litter on the shores of Little Bay.
- A *Gold Star Banner* was presented to the Sutton family after a 22-year delay. Karl J."Tex" Sutton was killed in a U.S. Navy training mission in 1988.
- Jackie Baird, local author, published *Annie's Portion*, her first novel.
- The Aquarium at Rockport Harbor welcomed its 50,000th Visitor.
- The ACISD hosted Gerda Weissman Klein, World-Renowned Holocaust Survivor.
- The TMM received a $100,000 gift from the O'Connor and Hewitt Foundation. The Maritime Collections and Education Center bears the name of the Foundation.
- L3Outdoors opened a Hog Hunting Business. Josh and Krystal White, owners, were featured in early 2011 on Discovery Channel's *Hogs Gone Wild*.

# 30 YEARS THROUGH THE NEWS/LENS

- The American Civil Liberties Union targeted the Town of Fulton's Nativity Scene at Fulton Navigation Park.
- C.J. Wax was the lone Rockport Mayoral Candidate on the ballot to replace the retiring Todd Pearson. No election was required.
- The TMM unveiled its exhibit, *Harold Phenix: Landscapes, Lighthouses & Longhorns*.
- AC Commissioners approved calling a Venue Tax Election for an Aquarium Education Center, a convention center, and a visitor's center. If approved, visitors would pay an additional two percent on their bill for overnight stays.
- Dr. H.F. Elliot, 85, the second full-time doctor in Rockport, who also made house calls, passed away.
- MP wrote a column calling for a protected left turn signal at the intersection of Business SH 35 and Henderson Street. It is the only major intersection on the highway without a protected turn signal. *There is still no protected left turn signal at that intersection.*

**APRIL**
- Farnsworth and Associates was involved in the season premier of *Extreme Makeover*.
- A golf tournament at RCC raised $34,000 for the ACEMS.
- Ground was broken on Shell Crete Square, Leadership Aransas County Class XIV's Class Project. *It is located north of the Aransas Pathways pavilion and bridge.*
- Rick McLester turned in his badge after 32 years of service in AC Law Enforcement.
- Jeff and Anne Bergstrom Hunt, the new owners of the Fulton-Bruhl Home located at 409 Broadway, renovated the structure to continue its historical integrity.

## 2010: YEAR TWENTY SEVEN

- Sazon Studio and Gallery opened.
- The AC Airport received TxDOT's *Most Improved Airport Award*.
- Diversified Wellness Association, LLC announced it was building a $1.6 million, 12,000-square-foot Urgent Care Facility on land between the new and old Walmart buildings.
- The Texas Ornithological Society held its spring meeting in AC. Its 200 attendees enjoyed bird watching in the Rockport-Fulton area.
- The local Hampton Inn & Suites earned *The Connie Award* as one of top eight hotels in the chain.
- It was announced the Town of Fulton would be installing 10 new streetlights in downtown Fulton.

**MAY**

- Collin Thompson was chosen as the winner of the inaugural *Symphony Guild of Corpus Christi Award for Music Composition*.
- The TPWD proposed purchasing the Big Tree Ranch in Lamar.
- Jimmy Kendrick won a seat on the Fulton Town Council by one vote. Later canvassing revealed he won by six votes. *Kendrick is now Mayor of the Town of Fulton.*
- AC voters rejected two of the three Propositions in the Venue Tax Election. The conference center and visitor's center were voted down, but the Aquarium Education Center was approved.
- The Memorial Heliport, located behind the ACEMS' new facility, was dedicated in honor of Dr. G.M. Pattillo, the organization's first medical director.
- Pleas from the public called for keeping the Community Pool open year around.

# 30 YEARS THROUGH THE NEWS/LENS

- The new Navy Junior Reserve Officers Training Corps (NJROTC) was established at RFHS.
- Vandals adjusted valves of the community pool causing most of the water to drain out.
- The Rockport Roadrunners, Youth Birding Team, identified 124 different species of birds to win first place in the Rough-wings Division of the *Great Texas Birding Classic.*
- Todd Pearson, retiring Rockport Mayor, was honored and "roasted" at a reception.
- Dr. Fred Warren closed his office after 30 years due to health reasons, but continued to serve as the Medical Director of the ACEMS.
- AC residents living in Bahia Bay, City by the Sea, and LaBuena Vida received support from AC Commissioners in their fight against the City of Aransas Pass' plan to annex those areas.
- The Rockport City Council approved spending $40,000 for a demonstration project showing an example of one of the new corners in downtown Rockport.

## JUNE

- Leases at Cove Harbor were the targets of a study. ACND Commissioners learned it would take a number of years to bring all Cove Harbor leases up to fair market value.
- George W. Fulton's 200th Birthday was celebrated at the Fulton Mansion.
- Kris Marshall signed a letter of intent to play baseball with the Los Angeles Angels.
- Work on the City of Rockport's new Water Transmission Line along the SH 35 bypass neared completion. *The project is supposed to satisfy water supply needs through 2030.*
- The RFCC received 5-star accreditation, the highest level

## 2010: YEAR TWENTY SEVEN

The RFCC achieved 5-Star accreditation in June 2010.

offered by the U.S. Chamber of Commerce.

- Thirty-nine brown pelicans and other birds were released at the ANWR after being rescued from the BP Oil Spill off the coast of New Orleans. *Bird releases in the Coastal Bend continued throughout the year.*
- Sugar Shack opened.
- A headline in RP read, "New causeway bid let this year; New causeway bridge in four years".
- The Bay Education Center opened.

Brown pelicans and other birds rescued from the BP Oil Spill were transferred to the ANWR.

# 30 YEARS THROUGH THE NEWS/LENS

The Bay Education Center opened to the public in June 2010.

- Surf Court Motel was demolished.
- The Texas Association of School Bus Technicians named David Anthony, a 20-plus-year Employee of the ACISD, *Shop Supervisor of the Year.*

**JULY**
- A large number of black skimmer fledglings were killed when vandals drove into the nesting area inside the circle drive at the end of Rockport Beach Park. The Aransas Bird and Nature Club offered a $1,000 reward to find the vandals.
- Pete Chamberlain was named *Citizen of the Year* at the RFCC's Annual Banquet.

The Surf Court Motel was demolished, making room for the south groin project.

- Chayla Garza received a full scholarship to play volleyball at Midland College.
- A Seguin man lost his arm in a boating accident after he was ejected and then run over by the boat.
- State Rep. Todd Hunter shared his thoughts about the Cruise Industry coming to Corpus Christi.
- MP wrote a column under the headline, "Who will operate Beach Park in 2012?"
- Oopsie Daisy Flowers opened.
- Capt. Tommy Moore and Evelyn Atkinson collaborated to complete *The Lobstick Prince: A Whooping Crane Story*, a book about a pair of Whooping Cranes and their devotion to their offspring.
- The Fulton Town Council considered expanding the Paws and Taws Convention Center.
- A toddler was found dead in a vehicle. The state took custody of the three other minor children of Cody Hickey and Kristie Bills.
- MP wrote a column about his oldest daughter's wedding to Doug Wilson.

**AUGUST**
- Don Hanks, a longtime local banker, went to work at ValueBank Texas.
- Wayne Oakman, former FVFD chief, was laid to rest with an Official Fireman's Funeral Service.
- An AC Resolution called for the two percent Venue Tax to go into effect October 1.
- Avelina Pina received special recognition in an AC Historical Society Contest, which sought the person who was born in Rockport and lived here the longest.

# 30 YEARS THROUGH THE NEWS/LENS

- ❏ The Texas Commission on Environmental Quality voted to allow discharge from the City of Rockport's Wastewater Treatment Plant to be released into Little Bay.
- ❏ The City of Rockport celebrated its 140th Birthday with a celebration complete with a birthday cake and citizens dressed in period costumes.
- ❏ A wind sculpture for the corner of Austin and Main Streets was commissioned by the City of Rockport in honor of former Mayor Todd Pearson's Vision and Support of a Revitalized Downtown.
- ❏ The Rockport City Council approved increasing its utility surcharge from $1.25 to $1.35 to help fund the Rockport, Fulton and Lamar VFDs.
- ❏ Fulton officials took the opportunity to show off the new downtown improvements, including new benches, a parking lot, cobblestone crosswalks, and on-street parking. *Keep Fulton Funky* t-shirts were distributed.

*Keep Fulton Funky* t-shirts were distributed during a RFCC Business After Hours during which Town of Fulton officials showed off the Town's downtown improvements.

**SEPTEMBER**
- ❏ A dolphin calf was rescued in Copano Bay by Team Marine

Mammal Stranding Network, a group of SeaWorld Veterinarians.
- Msgr. Louis Kihneman was appointed Vicar General for the Corpus Christi diocese.
- Lillian Penick, a former RFHS student, was hired as an ACISD Police Officer.
- Diane Probst earned her Certified Chamber Executive (CCE) designation, the highest professional certification awarded by American Chamber of Commerce Executives.
- The Fulton Town Council approved driving golf carts on Fulton Streets as long as certain requirements were met.
- The Texas Forest Service gave vaccinations to the Champion Western Soapberry Tree located at the home of Diane Tucker.
- Trey Little of Rockport broke a 37-year-old record with his tuna and blue marlin catch in the *White Marlin Open*.

Los Amigos Restaurant was demolished in September 2010. The sign remains standing on Business SH 35.

# 30 YEARS THROUGH THE NEWS/LENS

- Betty Williams, RFMS Principal, was selected *Education Service Center, Region 2, Principal of the Year.*
- Dr. Earl Matthews, an official of Aransas First, asked ACISD trustees to consider having a "living laboratory" on the property behind the Community Aquatic Park.
- Bill Mills, AC Sheriff, reported the tick problem at the animal shelter was under control.
- Robert A. Nelson Jr. of Rockport won $1 million in the Powerball Lottery with a ticket purchased at the Speedy Stop in Lamar.
- The RP van was involved in a rollover accident on SH 35 N., when returning from press in Port Lavaca. The total load of newspapers was destroyed. They had to be reprinted, but were delivered on time the next day.
- Denise Mendez, 20, of Rockport was found in the middle of the highway in front of Hampton Inn. She was declared dead at a Corpus Christi Hospital.
- A fire on the *Jimmy T* shrimp boat in Fulton Harbor kept fire fighters busy.

**OCTOBER**

- The RFCC bought the building across the street from its former location on Broadway Street for $235,000.
- Clint Edmundson was killed in a head-on collision on SH 35 N. just north of the AC Airport.
- Local officials took a trip to Cedar Bayou. The need to reopen Cedar Bayou, the fish pass between St. Joseph and Matagorda Islands, had been an issue for almost three decades.
- The RVFD celebrated its 125th Anniversary.
- Karl and Carol Hoepfner, *Whataburger's Biggest Fans*, set

## 2010: YEAR TWENTY SEVEN

a goal of visiting every Whataburger Restaurant in the U.S.
- AC Commissioners approved Tyler Technologies Software as a service to be used for AC's Judicial Criminal Information.
- The Rockport City Council re-funded bonds and saved taxpayers $286,000.

### NOVEMBER

- The first "historic" sign of the *Visionaries in Preservation Program* was installed at Shellcrete Square, next to Tule Creek, just north of Walmart.
- Almost half of AC's registered voters cast ballots in the November election.
- TxDOT informed the City of Rockport that it would need to pay up to $500,000 for the relocation of utilities due to the widening of SH 35 N.
- MP wrote a column about his youngest daughter receiving her Aggie ring.
- New playground equipment was installed at Memorial Park.
- Guy Grover resigned as ACISD athletic director and head football coach.
- AC Commissioners approved funding to study the Aransas Pathways Concept.
- Funding was received to construct an eight-foot tall fence around the AC Airport.

### DECEMBER

- Lamar Story, ACND Incumbent Commissioner, filed an ethics complaint against Tony Dominguez, newly elected AC Commissioner.
- AC Commissioners contributed $100,000 from its HOT reserves for the RFCC's new Visitor's Center.

# 30 YEARS THROUGH THE NEWS/LENS

- The RP offered its new E-edition online.
- The design for the City of Rockport's Community Center, the Gathering Place, was approved. *Due to funding issues, it was never built.*
- RK's Style Team opened.

## JANUARY

- A manatee was seen in a canal near Front Street in Lamar. It was later found dead.
- AC purchased 10 acres near Henderson Street with funds from a General Land Office Grant. The land will be held for conservation.
- A brief, but powerful thunderstorm uprooted trees in Old Rockport.
- The Rockport City Council approved an ordinance regulating the operation of golf carts and neighborhood electric vehicles on City Streets.
- The ACND approved converting a boat slip in Rockport Harbor into a covered deck where the public can rest.
- The remaining bulbouts in downtown Rockport were being updated and stained a rust color.
- The copper wiring in the Saltwater Pavilion was stolen.
- ACISD Trustees called for another School Bond Election, which requested $26.8 million to renovate Fulton and Live Oak Learning Centers.
- MP wrote a column about his 30-year reunion at Texas A&M and his college experiences with the Three Musketeers, his two roommates and himself.

## FEBRUARY

- The Texas Academy of Sciences named Martha McLeod, Fulton Learning Center teacher, as *Outstanding Texas Educator*.

# 30 YEARS THROUGH THE NEWS/LENS

Nine historic signs, a product of the *Visionaries in Preservation Program*, were ready to be installed.

- The ACISD was named one of three school districts as State-wide Finalists for the prestigious *HEB Excellence Award*.
- Nine unique historic signs were being prepared for installation as part of the *Visionaries in Preservation Program*.
- Rockport Urgent Care Center opened.
- Two accidents occurred almost simultaneously on SH 35 bypass overpasses when a winter storm brought freezing rain and overpasses were frozen. During this ice event, the importance of emergency medical facilities, located north of the harbor bridge, was brought into prominence. Because the harbor bridge was closed due to being frozen, the EMS couldn't transport individuals to hospitals in Corpus Christi.
- Huey Chancellor was hired as the new ACISD athletic director and head football coach.
- The Daughters of the Republic of Texas announced the

historic Fulton Schoolhouse would be converted into a museum.
- Local, state and federal authorities discovered a methamphetamine lab in a motor home behind a house on Portia Avenue.
- State Rep. Todd Hunter was appointed to chair the powerful Texas Calendars Committee.
- The City of Rockport placed rocks along portions of the Little Bay Shoreline to prevent further erosion.
- The Friends of the Pool group received its nonprofit designation and opened its doors to new programs and projects at the pool.
- The Fulton Town Council approved an Employee Retirement Plan.
- The Rockport City Council debated where to locate a proposed community garden. *A piece of land at the south end of Mathis Park was eventually chosen for the site.*

## MARCH
- Betsy Farmer, Ben Marshall, and Marissa Kuertz were named to the UIL All-State Choir.
- Crystal Riley, Esai Salazar, John Dupnik, and Bryan Nguyen were named to the UIL All-State Band.
- The RFHS Lady Pirate varsity basketball team won the Regional Tournament and advanced to State. Their magical season ended with a loss in the State Semifinals.
- Mary John Lynch received the *Julius Zinn Seniors' Service Award* at the Tennis Hall of Fame Recognition and USTA-USPTA Awards Banquet.
- AC Commissioners purchased additional land on Mimosa and Concho Streets for a future courthouse.

# 30 YEARS THROUGH THE NEWS/LENS

The RFHS Lady Pirates received a big sendoff on their way to the State Basketball Tournament.

- The hospital in Aransas Pass, under new ownership, was renamed Care Regional Medical Center.
- Chris Bently, RFHS head girl's basketball coach, was named *District 30-3A Coach of the Year*.
- Erika Williams was named to the UIL State All-Tournament Team.
- The City of Rockport considered accepting a large art collection from the estate of Cora T. Keeler.
- While dancing, Cheyenne Cyr Turner, member of the RFHS NJROTC, collapsed at the NJROTC Ball. The DJ performed CPR, but she died later that evening.
- A Venue Tax Election was called to fund the Aransas Pathways Project. *Since the Venue Tax was passed, numerous Pathways' projects have been funded for the betterment of AC.*
- Dan Gill launched *Pelagic*, the boat he spent several years building.

## 2011: YEAR TWENTY EIGHT

Dan Gill launched *Pelagic*, a boat he built from scratch.

- Storm water projects totaling $15.4 million were prioritized and presented in the Stormwater Management Plan.
- Jason Culver, Army Specialist, surprised Caroline Atkins, his mother, when he returned home from Afghanistan on leave.
- Jeff Steckler and Jimmy Lloyd brought home the $25,000 first place prize in the *Redfish Series Tournament* held in Chalmette, LA.
- K-Bob's Steakhouse moved into the old Chili's Restaurant in front of Walmart.

## APRIL

- Jane DeDecker, Colorado sculptor, poured saltwater on her artwork, *Into the Wind*, during dedication ceremonies at the RCA Sculpture Garden.
- The RFCC offered its old building to the ACND. The ACND tabled action on the matter, but in July accepted the building as is.

# 30 YEARS THROUGH THE NEWS/LENS

- Hayley Grosjean signed a letter of intent to compete in track at Angelo State University.
- Jackie Longino's Hog was named *Reserve Breed Champion* at the Houston Livestock Show and Rodeo.
- TPWD awarded Ed Hegen a 40-year Service Award.
- Glenda Burdick, former Rockport Mayor, was given the *Mason's Community Builder Award*.
- Jad Smith, Chief Appraiser for the AC Appraisal District, retired after 30 years of service.
- Tommy Moore, ACND Chairman, notified the City of Rockport the ACND did not intend to renew the agreement with the City for the operation of the Beach Park.
- Bob Hewes, former AC Sheriff, passed away, marking the end of an era.

**MAY**

- John Jackson's Family History was told in his new book, *Taking the Tide; My Family's Ebb and Flow in Rockport, Texas*.
- Martha McLeod, science teacher at Fulton Learning Center, was one of 85 mathematics and science teachers in the nation named as a recipient of the prestigious *Presidential Award for Excellence in Mathematics and Science Teaching*. McLeod flew to Washington to receive her award.
- MP wrote a column celebrating the death of Osama bin Laden, but warned the threat of terrorism will continue, and may even get worse.
- The historical marker for the Sorenson-Stair building was unveiled, coinciding with the grand reopening of the Estelle Stair Gallery. *During a seven-year restoration project, the building was remodeled to its original design.*

- The Youth Team won the *Birding Classic* identifying 143 species in one day, the second consecutive win for the team.
- Logan Jasek, RFMS student, placed second at the *Texas State History Day Competition* and 10th place in the nation at the *National History Day Competition*.
- Ground was broken on the long-awaited Fulton Mansion Visitors' Center.
- MP wrote a column about his youngest daughter graduating from college, and the impending empty nest.
- Hayley Grosjean placed fourth in discus and fifth in shot put at the UIL State Track Meet.
- Descendants of Adolph L. Bracht and Gertrude Prophet Bracht, original owners of the home at 409 N. Magnolia Street, attended the unveiling of the home's historical marker.
- The Grog Bar opened.

**JUNE**

- Howard Murph, AC Commissioner, suddenly passed away.
- Glow Restaurant opened.
- The Rockport Music Festival at Fulton Navigation Park featured Texas Legends Guy Clark, Ray Wylie Hubbard, and Jerry Jeff Walker.
- AC was ranked 46th out of 254 counties in terms of travel spending.
- Seaworthy Marine received the *Blue Ribbon Award* in Washington, DC at the U.S. Chamber of Commerce Small Business Summit.
- Two of three planned bike racks were placed in downtown Rockport.
- The ACEMS sought a 10 percent increase in funding from government entities in AC.

# 30 YEARS THROUGH THE NEWS/LENS

- ❏ The Rockport City Council approved the $2.8 million bid from Barcom Commercial to build its service center complex on the SH 35 bypass. *It now houses the City's Public Works and Building Departments.*
- ❏ ACND Commissioners approved a $965,000 bid to build the Breakwater Pier on the south end of Rockport Harbor. The remaining concrete rubble from the old Surf Court Motel was used for the base of the breakwater pier.
- ❏ Bobby Jackson, RFMS Texas History Teacher, played the role of Enrique Esparza, a survivor of the Alamo, during a production at the 102th annual Daughters of the Republic of Texas Convention.
- ❏ Russel Cole, Fulton Mayor, was appointed to the Precinct 4 AC Commissioner's post vacated upon the death of Howard Murph.
- ❏ The Daily Grind Coffee Shop moved to its new location across the street from its original location in downtown Rockport.

**JULY**

- ❏ Airport Park, directly behind the airport, was renamed *Howard Murph Memorial Park* in honor of the late AC Commissioner who was instrumental in the park's creation.
- ❏ The Rockport City Council heard a proposal for a bungee jump ride at Rockport Beach Park. *The ride was never installed.*
- ❏ Augie Garcia and Johnny Rios, local umpires, called games in the State Little League Tournament.
- ❏ Father Joseph Thang Nguyen, formerly of Rockport, was ordained as a Catholic Priest.
- ❏ Jimmy Kendrick was appointed Fulton's new mayor.

Airport Park was renamed Howard Murph Park in honor of the late AC Commissioner.

- Carla Reed was named *Citizen of the Year* at the RFCC's annual banquet.
- The Aransas Pathways Steering Committee was created by county resolution.
- Tom Blazek, Rockport City Manager, announced his retirement.
- Ricky Littleton was selected as TxDOT AC Maintenance Office Supervisor.
- ACISD Trustees ended the RFHS Swim Program.
- Two self-contained aquarium units were purchased by the Coastal Bend Community Foundation and dedicated at the Aquarium at Rockport Harbor.
- The Rockport, Fulton and Lamar VFDs gave the Big Tree in Lamar a hefty drink of water to help the trophy oak better weather the current drought conditions.
- State Sen. Glenn Hegar sent a letter to the Texas Attorney General questioning the ACND's ability to operate and maintain the Rockport Beach Park, as well as its ability to finance such operations with tax money.

## AUGUST

- The Cedar Bayou dredging permit was finally received. *Work on opening Cedar Bayou and Vinson Slough began in 2014.*

# 30 YEARS THROUGH THE NEWS/LENS

- AC Commissioners issued $5.5 million in bonds for Storm Water Projects.
- Aransas Bay Real Estate opened.
- Construction on the new Copano Causeway began.
- The new RFCC and Visitors' Center opened.
- The ACND planted more palm trees along the front of the festival grounds.
- Les "Googles" Cole was appointed to fill Jimmy Kendrick's Alderman position after Kendrick was appointed mayor of Fulton.
- AC Commissioners approved a new redistricting map for AC's four precincts.
- A home at 16 Nassau in Key Allegro was destroyed by fire. A second home sustained severe damage.
- Pat Daly retired, ending his 27-year career as a Justice of the Peace.

A huge crowd was on hand for the opening of the RFCC's new offices and Visitors' Center.

## 2011: YEAR TWENTY EIGHT

## SEPTEMBER

- ❏ MP wrote a column about the Bastrop wildfire and how close it hit to home. His aunt and uncle lost everything when the blaze began a short distance from their home and rental properties.
- ❏ Diana McGinnis filled the unexpired term of Precinct 2 Justice of the Peace vacated by retiring Judge Pat Daly.
- ❏ On the 10th Anniversary of the 9/11 Terrorist Attacks, AC remembered those who were lost.
- ❏ The Rockport City Council approved a bid to construct the Tule Hike and Bike Trail after a 10-1/2 year journey. TxDOT later rejected the bid.
- ❏ Patricia Chapman's song, *Love Can Live for Always*, was the winner in a United Kingdom Lyrics Contest.
- ❏ The ACND gave a report about dealings with the Bass family regarding property line changes on the Rockport Harborfront Property.
- ❏ Cell phone service was out for almost six hours, highlighting our dependency on such devices.
- ❏ Ground was broken for the new Aquarium Education Center, the first Venue Tax Project.
- ❏ The AC Historical Society signed an agreement to

On the 10th anniversary of 9-11, AC remembered.

# 30 YEARS THROUGH THE NEWS/LENS

Ground was broken in October 2011 for the Aquarium Education Center, the first Venue Tax Project.

be custodians of the Bruhl-Paul-Johnson house. AC owns the house and the property on which it sits.
- Africanized bees attacked and killed three family dogs.
- Paula Bell, Fulton Postmaster, retired.

**OCTOBER**
- John Solis served as Umpire at the Southwest Regional Little League Baseball Tournament during the game between New Mexico and Louisiana.
- The Fulton-Bruhl House was rededicated after extensive renovations.
- The AC Historical Society sought a place to relocate the Bruhl-Paul-Johnson House.
- Ground was broken for the new building of the Humane Society and Adoption Center of Rockport-Fulton.
- The Community Garden at Mathis Park began operation.
- A robbery at Rockport Bakery was thwarted when Patrick

## 2011: YEAR TWENTY EIGHT

Garza struck the robber with a mixing bowl and knocked the suspect to the ground. In the melee, the robber grabbed the cash register, but it was jerked out of his hands because it was still plugged in. The robber was held until the RPD arrived.

- Historical documents of 1858 Land Grants of AC were found at the Taft Museum.
- The RFHS Band earned Superior Ratings at UIL Competition for the fifth consecutive year.
- Cash raised through fundraising for the Emerald Drill Team to attend the Macy's Thanksgiving Day Parade in NYC was never deposited. An investigation began. *Crystal Simmons, 32, an employee of ACISD, was arrested in connection with the missing money.*
- Dr. Neva Kelly, ACISD assistant superintendent, received the *Texas Association of Gifted and Talented Administrator of the Year Award.*
- Mary Lucille Jackson, former RCA director, passed away.

## NOVEMBER

- Two people were killed and a third was seriously injured when the Harbor View Apartments in downtown Rockport caught fire in the middle of the night. Tenants were trapped in their apartments and some were able to jump from the second floor to safety.
- A YouTube video showing William Adams, AC Court-At-Law Judge, beating Hillary Adams, his daughter, went viral. It was viewed more than 3 million times. State and National media descended on AC.
- MP wrote a column under the headline "Adams should give up his judge's post." *Adams never resigned, but was defeated*

# 30 YEARS THROUGH THE NEWS/LENS

Two people were killed in the fire at the Harbor View Apartments.

*in the 2014 GOP Primary election by Richard Bianchi, AC Attorney.*

- The Rockport City Council formally declined the Keeler Art Collection. *A decision was made to pass the collection to the Corpus Christi Art Museum due to not finding a suitable location nor being able to fund future security, conservation and restoration costs.*
- Construction began on Habitat for Humanity's seventh home.
- Rudy Ruettiger, Notre Dame graduate and subject of the movie, *Rudy*, signed autographs at a Rockport-Fulton Youth Football event.
- An arrest warrant was issued for Lewis S. Robinson III, Key Allegro Sales LLC owner, for theft over $20,000, but under $100,000.
- A temporary restraining order hearing was held regarding parental custody for the 10-year-old daughter of Judge

Williams Adams and Hallie Adams. News crews hung around all day just to get a shot of the judge. He was later granted visitation with his daughter under supervision.
- The RCA unveiled its newest sculpture *White Walking Flower*, a recent work by James Surls, American sculptor.
- Marine Wix, former longtime AC Treasurer, passed away.
- Camp Aranzazu celebrated the opening of its new Health Center.

## DECEMBER

- Dr. Gary Gilbert and Rita, his wife, donated land at the corner of Cedar and Church Streets for historical preservation purposes. *The Bruhl-Paul-Johnson house was moved to that property, remodeled, and is now the home of the History Center for Aransas County.*
- Fulton Community Church, Fulton's first church, received its historical marker.
- Kevin Carruth, of Paris, TX, was selected as Rockport's new City Manager.
- Coastal Bend Health Foods opened.
- Construction on the Fulton Mansion's Education and History Center was stalled for a few months as a new contractor was secured. Richard Dias Construction went to the site to cover the roof and clean up the site in the interim.
- Dr. Thomas McKinley, MD, passed away after a sudden illness.
- Jeff Dinger, owner of the Cinema 4 Theater, announced plans to transform the old HEB building into a Bistro Cinema to include six theaters with food service and lease space for merchants. *Dinger later decided not to build the Bistro Cinema.*

# 30 YEARS THROUGH THE NEWS/LENS

- A press conference was held to announce the new *Warriors Weekend Heroes Cup Fishing Tournament* to be held in September 2012.
- Leadership Aransas County Class XVI received approval to build a Dog Park in Memorial Park as its class project.
- The Tule Hike and Bike Trail groundbreaking was held.
- After serving a year in Kabul, Charles Douglas Olsen, Specialist-4, returned home from Afghanistan.
- A Christmas Eve fire gutted the home of Bill and Margaret Brown. Roland Rodriguez gave Margaret a motorized electric wheelchair to replace the one lost in the fire.
- The City of Rockport hired an Austin law firm to assist in negotiating with the ACND regarding the Rockport Beach Park.
- The Fulton Town Council approved changes for the lighting of the Fulton Pier.

## 2012: YEAR TWENTY NINE

### JANUARY

- The Aquarium at Rockport Harbor received a new friend and benefactor, Timothy Tristan, DVM of Corpus Christi. Tristan performed surgery on a creole fish and helped Marley, the Morey Eel. *He is now an aquarium board member.*
- Key Allegro Real Estate honored Wynell McLain for 45 years of service.
- Pam Stanley, local artist, was shot and killed by her estranged husband before he turned the gun on himself.
- The Pirate Store opened.
- Travis Threadgill, 40, of Rockport, and two Port Lavaca men were killed in a fiery head-on crash on SH 35, between

Local artist David Allgood worked day and night on the Big Blue Crab.

# 30 YEARS THROUGH THE NEWS/LENS

Holiday Beach and Cavasso Creek. The trucks burst into flames upon impact.

- A discussion regarding which governmental group would manage the Rockport Beach Park drew a large crowd at the RFCC Luncheon.

- David Allgood, local artist, worked day and night to recreate the old landmark, the Big Blue Crab. *The completed crab is now located at the south end of the Ski Basin.*

- Ground was broken on the new chapel of the Rockport Branch of the Church of Jesus Christ of Latter Day Saints.

- After a complaint was made regarding campaign contributions, the Ethics Commission fined Tony Dominguez $1,000 and Derrick Construction Co. $500.

- Hammerheads Bar and Grill opened. *Rusty's Tropical Grill is now in that location.*

- Camp Aranzazu was certified as a Wildlife Habitat.

- The Fulton Town Council approved spending $20,000 for painting and floor repairs at the Paws and Taws Convention Center.

- AC Commissioners hired Richard Thompson to oversee Venue Tax Projects.

- Ground was broken on the new Live Oak Learning Center.

- Larry Sinclair, RPD Lt., David Rollins, Patrolman, and Albert Howie, RVFD Chief, were given *Lifesaver Awards* for their courageous acts during the fire at the Harbor Apartments in downtown Rockport.

- Joschlyn Edwards, RFHS NJROTC Cadet, received a full four-year scholarship from the Navy ROTC.

- The Rockport City Council stopped the progress on building the *Gathering Place*, a community center, next to the Community Aquatic Park.

## FEBRUARY

- James Cooper-Hill, local attorney, published his book, *Miranda Warning*.
- Shelly Stuart, RFCC's Vice President of Operations, graduated from the Institute for Organization Management.
- MP wrote a column calling on the ACND to work as soon as possible with the General Land Office and the Bass family to "line up" the individual parcels of property, which make up the Rockport harbor front.
- By the Bay Chiropractic opened.
- The RFHS Lady Pirates basketball team lost to West Oso in UIL Area Playoffs.
- The Rockport Computer Group celebrated its 25th Anniversary.

## MARCH

- In a press conference held outside its office, the ACND announced it would take over operations of Rockport Beach.
- The Fulton Pier went green with new LED lighting on the pier and in the water.
- Brittany Renee Tristan, 22, a local resident, was killed in a two vehicle head-on collision on SH 35 outside of Gregory.
- The late Delo Caspary and the late Willie Close were inducted into the TMM's *Perry R. Bass Memorial Sports Fishing Wall of Fame*.
- Marshawn O'Neal Herron, RFMS coach, was arrested for indecency with a child.
- State Rep. Geanie Morrison and Congressman Blake Farenthold were AC's newest state and national lawmakers.

# 30 YEARS THROUGH THE NEWS/LENS

- Groundbreaking ceremonies were held for the new History Center for Aransas County at 801 E. Cedar Street.
- A winter Texan from Canada was hit and killed, while walking across Market Street at night.

**APRIL**

- The Aquarium at Rockport Harbor's Education Center was officially opened.
- Juanita L. Wagley, the first lady of Rockport Real Estate, passed away.
- The Rockport City Council agreed to sell all equipment and material used for maintenance at Rockport Beach Park to the ACND for $45,349.
- AC Commissioners approved the Stormwater Management Plan.
- J&M Air Conditioning changed its' name to Aire Serv of the Coastal Bend.
- The RFHS band won its fifth consecutive UIL Concert and Sight Reading Contest Sweepstakes Award.
- The new AgriLife Extension Complex off Airport Road opened.
- ACISD Trustees began researching natural gas conversion for school buses. The City of Rockport also considered the conversion for City vehicles.
- The RFHS Theatre Department's One-Act play, *The Theatre of Illusion,* advanced to UIL State Contest The drama team students finished second runner up.

**MAY**

- The TMM's new Collections and Education Center was dedicated.

## 2012: YEAR TWENTY NINE

A new sign was posted at Rockport Beach announcing the tourist attraction is now operated by the ACND. The City of Rockport ran Rockport Beach Park for the previous 25 years.

- RFHS Family and Consumer Science teachers were awarded $75,000 from the ACISD Education Foundation for the Culinary Arts Program.
- Jim Edler and Tiffanie Hoover participated in the Rotary Group Study Exchange Program in the Philippines.
- Kevin Johnson approached the ACND about placing an inflatable water slide near the Bay Education Center at the entrance of the Rockport Beach. *No decision was made during a resident packed meeting.*
- Cantwell's Classic Cars opened in the old Sonic location. *The business has since moved to a location on the SH 35 bypass.*
- Stratton Williams signed a letter of intent to play basketball at Dallas Baptist University.
- New Wayfinding Signs were unveiled by C.J. Wax, Rockport Mayor, and Jimmy Kendrick, Fulton Mayor.
- Saltwater Flats RV Park opened.
- Morgan Hale signed a letter of intent to play basketball at the University of Texas at Tyler.

# 30 YEARS THROUGH THE NEWS/LENS

The mayors of Rockport and Fulton unveiled new Wayfinding Signs.

❏ Darren Pham signed a letter of intent to play football at Howard Payne University.
❏ A large tree branch fell across Alamito Street in old Rockport. Because it occurred during the night, Rockport and Fulton VFDs supplied lighting so that City of Rockport crews could remove the debris from the roadway.
❏ Chartroom restaurant opened.

**JUNE**

❏ Bill Mills, AC Sheriff, received 73.91 percent of the vote against two opponents in the GOP Primary Election.
❏ Betty Stiles defeated Russel Cole, incumbent Precinct 4 AC Commissioner, by three votes in the GOP Primary election.
❏ An additional 170 acres of Whooping Crane Habitat was acquired in a coordinated effort by the Coastal Bend Bays & Estuaries Foundation, the Whooping Crane Conservation Association, and the TPWD.
❏ Betty Stiles was chosen at the Texas State GOP Convention to represent Congressional District 27 in the Electoral College when it convened in December.

## 2012: YEAR TWENTY NINE

- The ACISD Education Foundation dedicated the Community in Art Project in front of the Martha Luigi Auditorium.
- The First Call Alert System replaced the old Reverse 911 system.
- The Dog Park at Memorial Park opened with about two acres of fenced land including areas for large and small dogs. Leadership Aransas County Class XVI raised more than $50,000 to build the park.

The Dog Park at Memorial Park is the Leadership Aransas County Class XVI class project.

- Pirates Landing announced it would offer a gathering place for youth at First Presbyterian Church's Miriam Ferrell Youth Center.
- Bradley Becker earned the rank of Eagle Scout.
- Leadership AC Class XVI graduated 19 leaders, the largest class in the history of the program.
- Diane Probst, President and CEO of the RFCC, was awarded the *Marvin Hurley Award*, the Texas Chamber of Commerce Executives organization's highest award.

# 30 YEARS THROUGH THE NEWS/LENS

- Jake Manlove, RFMS student, won second place at the *National History Day Competition* in Washington, DC.

**JULY**

- Twenty Great Egret carcasses were located in a field next to Smile Brite Dental Center. The cause of death was unknown.

- Sergeant Nicholas MacLean, RFHS graduate, was awarded a Purple Heart after being wounded in Afghanistan.

Diane Probst, RFCC President/CEO, was awarded the Texas Chamber of Commerce Executives highest award in June 2012.

- A new ACISD standardized dress code for the fall semester was announced.

- The inaugural *Bastante John Uhr Memorial Billfish Tournament* awarded almost $186,000 in prizes, and donated approximately $50,000 to local charities.

- Susie Bracht Black displayed a wide array of fabric art during her first show at Wind Way Gallery.

- More than 35 area firefighters battled an oil tank fire across from Camp Aranzazu on FM 1781. Lightning was suspected as cause of the fire.

- The Lamar VFD began fundraising efforts for a new station

because the lease on its fire station was ending in 30 months.
- Jerry Lewis was named *Citizen of the Year* at the RFCC's annual banquet.
- J.D. Simpson was named Rotary District Governor. His father served as District Governor 50 years ago.
- The AC Airport received $715,000 from the Texas Transportation Commission for a fence to keep deer, coyotes, rabbits, raccoons and feral hogs off the runways.
- William Walston, Rockport City attorney, resigned after 24 years of service.
- AC Commissioners approved the purchase of the Linda S. Castro Property on SH 35 N. as a potential bird-viewing site.
- A prescription drug drop box was put into service in front of the AC Detention Center.

## AUGUST

- Diamonte Azul Day Spa opened.
- MP wrote a column about the death of Don Chandler, his first mentor in the newspaper business.
- Castaways unveiled a sign announcing the site of the thrift shop's new location on Market Street.
- John P. Jackson delivered the summer commencement address at his alma mater, Texas A&M University–Kingsville.
- Stripes announced it would build a new store at the northeast corner of Business SH 35 and Henderson Street.
- The History Center for Aransas County, the Bruhl-Paul-Johnson home, was moved to its permanent home on Cedar Street.
- Whataburger officials gave Karl and Carol Hoepfner a new minivan after the couple visited every U.S. Whataburger location.

# 30 YEARS THROUGH THE NEWS/LENS

People watched in awe as the house, which is now occupied by the History Center for AC, was moved.

- Gold Master Jewelers opened.
- The Fulton Mansion Education and History Center, located across the street behind the Mansion, was dedicated after more than a decade of planning and development.

**SEPTEMBER**

- The inaugural AquaFest was held to raise funds and awareness of the Aquarium at Rockport Harbor. It was held on the Aquarium's fifth Anniversary.
- William Adams, AC Court-At-Law Judge, received a public warning from the State Commission on Judicial Conduct as a result of him being seen on a video beating his daughter. His daughter uploaded the video on YouTube, creating a national uproar.
- AEP experienced equipment failure and 4,144 customers were without electrical power for about four hours.
- MP wrote a column about the Texas A&M Aggies' first SEC

Football Game played against the Florida Gators at Kyle Field. During that game, the football world was introduced to an unknown quarterback named Johnny Manziel, originally from Kerrville, Texas.
- The Humane Society and Adoption Center of Rockport-Fulton opened its new facility, House of Hope.
- World Beauty Emporium opened.
- A scavenger hunt was held to commemorate the 50th Anniversary of Key Allegro.
- Jessica Janota, RFMS eighth grade social studies teacher, was selected *Gulf Coast Area Rising Star Teacher of the Gifted*.

## OCTOBER

- The FVFD broke ground on its new fire station at 401 N. Ninth in Fulton.
- Plans for a new LaQuinta Hotel and Suites were announced.
- The inaugural Shopping Tournament was held as a fundraiser for the ACISD Education Foundation.
- The Big Tree Ranch became a new unit of Goose Island State Park.
- Victoria Moroles, daughter of Suzanna Moroles, Rockport native, and niece of Jesus Moroles, renowned sculptor, had a co-starring role in an episode of *CSI–Las Vegas*.
- Nostalgic photos of Key Allegro, *Then and Now*, were published in RP in celebration of the 50th anniversary of that iconic canal subdivision.
- Brent Douglass, John T. Davis and James R. Dennis, teamed up to write *This Slice of Life* under the pseudonym of Miles Arceneaux. The book was based in Rockport during the 1970s.

# 30 YEARS THROUGH THE NEWS/LENS

The 50th anniversary of Key Allegro was celebrated in 2012.

- All the towering pine trees on the property across SH 35 from HEB were removed due to disease. The trees were originally planted in the 40s. *Small pines have since been planted on that property.*
- The ACISD joined 87 school districts in a lawsuit against the state in regard to how schools are funded.
- The RFHS varsity volleyball team was undefeated in district play.
- Michael Contreras, Army Pfc., came home to visit his family.
- The Wilderness Trail in Memorial Park was opened.
- MP wrote a column about his reunion in Rockport with his Squadron 2 Classmates from his days at Texas A&M.

**NOVEMBER**

- The Rockport City Council accepted the sculpture, *Rockport Glory*, from an anonymous donor. The City placed the piece across from Little Bay, adjacent to McDonalds.
- Bill Mills was reelected AC Sheriff with almost 70 percent of the votes cast.
- The Baldwin-Brundrett Home received its historical marker.

## 2012: YEAR TWENTY NINE

- Israel Rubalcaba, Aransas County *Go Texan Committee*, was honored at the Houston Livestock Show and Rodeo as *Rookie Ambassador of the Year*.
- Felicia Cypress, Army Tech Sergeant, surprised her daughters when she came home early from a seven-month deployment.
- Danny Boehm was ordained a Deacon in the Sacred Heart Catholic Church.

**DECEMBER**

- The City of Rockport received the *President's Award* from the Coastal Bend Bays Foundation.
- The *Today in America* TV show filmed segments about Rockport and Fulton, which aired nationally. Terry Bradshaw, Hall of Fame NFL Quarterback, narrated it.
- Texas Farm Bureau Insurance opened.
- The City of Rockport officially opened the Tule Hike and Bike Trail for public use.
- The tragic school shooting in Connecticut raised attention about school safety. Attorney General Greg Abbott published a list of 78 districts in the state non-compliant with school safety measures, which included the ACISD. ACISD disputed the claim. A communication gap was revealed between state agents and school districts, which caused the ACISD's poor report.
- Coastal Collision opened.
- Daniel Garcia, USMC Staff Sgt., made a surprise visit to Live Oak Learning Center to visit Alana Garcia, his daughter. She had not seen her dad for six months.

# 30 YEARS THROUGH THE NEWS/LENS

## JANUARY

- A historical marker was unveiled at the Mills' Wharf original location.
- MP wrote a column about his miniature dachshund's successful emergency spinal surgery. Tucker was paralyzed, while running down the driveway right before MP's family celebrated Christmas.
- A Nesting Bird Advisory Group was established by the ACND to provide information about the protection of nesting birds at the Rockport Beach.
- The statue of *Mary and Baby Jesus* was installed and blessed by Bishop Michael Mulvey at St. Peter's Catholic Church on FM 1781. The statue had been moved from the shores on Fulton Beach Road by its owner and given to the church.
- 7-Eleven bought the three local Speedy Stop stores.
- The states' local Immunization Office closed, but it was announced residents could still receive immunizations twice weekly at the ACEMS building.
- A RFHS student started a fire in a boy's restroom. Personnel responded quickly and the student was taken into custody.
- The ACND stockpiled 1,200-1,600 yards of oyster shells at Cove Harbor to be used for the Live Oak Peninsula Shoreline Stabilization Project.
- The Coastal Task Force unveiled its plan to address the State Legislature regarding rising windstorm insurance costs.

## 2013: YEAR THIRTY

- AC Rural Rail District Representatives gave the AC Commissioners an update about the group. The district had to be formed in conjunction with San Patricio and Nueces Counties so that AC would not lose the rail system, which ran in front of the old Degussa Property on Business SH 35 S.
- Spanky's flagship liquor store opened.

**FEBRUARY**

- The ACND was awarded a $1.2 million grant to restore marsh habitat and to stabilize the shoreline of Little Bay along Broadway Street.
- The State's School Finance System was ruled unconstitutional. The ACISD was one of 88 school districts involved in the lawsuit against the State.
- The Town of Fulton created its own Police Department with Rick McLester as Chief of Police.
- Michael Welborn, former District Judge, was appointed new District Attorney for Aransas and San Patricio Counties.
- FM 1781 was renamed Highway 1781. It was later changed to Loop 1781.
- Irma Parker, Rockport City Secretary, resigned to become the City Secretary in Port Aransas.
- Kennah Leal signed a letter of intent to play soccer for the Texas A&M Corpus Christi Lady Islanders.
- Several Rockport Residents were on the Carnival Triumph cruise ship, which was towed to Mobile, AL after a fire in the diesel generator erupted and disabled the ship's power.
- Betty Baker, founder of the HummerBird Celebration, shared Connie Hagar's Legacy when the sign was unveiled at the Connie Hagar Cottage Sanctuary at First and Church Streets.
- Jim Remley, ACISD Board President, resigned.

# 30 YEARS THROUGH THE NEWS/LENS

- A juvenile Whooping Crane was shot and killed. Worthey Wiles of Dallas pled guilty. *He was ordered to pay a $5,000 fine, serve a one-year term of probation and make a $10,000 community service payment to the nonprofit organization Friends of Aransas and Matagorda Island National Wildlife Refuges.*
- A hunt was on for the suspect in the robbery of the Walmart IBC branch. Police from Rockport and Aransas Pass, the ACSO, and U.S. Marshalls arrested Christopher William Adams, 23, of Granbury, Texas.

**MARCH**

- Martha McLeod and Jessica Janota were named finalists for the *2013 HEB Excellence in Education Award*, recognizing them as among the best educators in Texas.
- A sign was unveiled during the dedication of the Big Blue Crab, now located on the south end of Little Bay. *The crab has become a tourist draw, very much like its predecessor in the 1950s, 60s and 70s.*

It was a big day when the Big Blue Crab was dedicated at the south end of the ski basin.

- A Federal Judge ruled in favor of The Aransas Project in its lawsuit against the State regarding freshwater inflows into the Whooping Cranes' Habitat.
- MP wrote another column about the need for a protected left turn signal at the intersection of Business SH 35 and Henderson Street.
- The RFHS Tennis Team placed third at the UIL State Tournament.
- Ground was broken on the LaQuinta Inn & Suites.
- Sea turtles were found at Rockport Beach. They died shortly after being rescued by personnel at the University of Texas Marine Science Institute.
- Jonette Childs and Jim Friebele were inducted into the TMM's *Perry R. Bass Memorial Sports Fishing Wall of Fame*.
- Jack Wright received the *Community Builder Award* from the Masonic Lodge.
- The Supreme Court refused to hear an appeal challenging the Texas Open Meetings Act, keeping the state law banning government officials from talking business in informal settings intact.

## APRIL

- Jimmy Kendrick, Fulton Mayor, gave Leslie "Googles" Cole the inaugural *Legacy Award*, a new watch, and proclaimed April 2 *"Googles" Cole Day* in Fulton.
- The RP unveiled its upgraded website.
- The Ivy Lane Birding and Nature Site opened in Peninsula Oaks. This site was the first Aransas Pathways Project to open.
- Luce Insurance moved to its new location on Market Street. *The former Sipe Real Estate complex at which Luce's business*

*was located has been demolished to make room for another convenience store.*
- The Stripes Convenience Store at the corner of Glass Avenue and Business SH 35 closed the same day that the new Stripes store opened at the intersection of Business SH 35 and Henderson Street.
- Martha McLeod, Fulton Learning Center teacher, was named to the *National Teachers Hall of Fame*.
- Diana McGinnis, Precinct 2 Justice of the Peace, discovered case records in municipal court, which were not properly filed.
- A historical marker for the TPWD Marine Lab at Rockport Harbor was dedicated.
- The RFHS Pirate Track Team won the UIL District Track Meet for the third consecutive year.
- Bennie Moore was attacked by a red-shouldered hawk, which was building a nest on her property.
- Alli McLain, RFHS tennis player, advanced to the UIL State Tournament.
- A new play structure was installed at Memorial Park.

**MAY**

- Rookery Island in San Antonio Bay was stripped of birds, nests, and eggs.
- MP wrote a column about the death of his father-in-law.
- Margaret's Mysteries Resale Shop opened at its new location across from Rockport City Hall. *This location was the former Rockport City Hall Annex building.*
- John Kroll, Navy Veteran, and April, his wife, were given a new home through the Navy Wounded Warrior Program.

## 2013: YEAR THIRTY

- Alex Fahrenthold won the silver medal in the 300-meter hurdles at the UIL State Track Meet.
- Mark Gilliam, former AC sheriff, was killed in a wreck near Houston.
- The Lamar VFD broke ground on its new fire station.
- Aransas Blaha and Olive Smith were crowned *Texas State Surfing Champions* in their respective categories.
- A self-guided historical audio tour was made available at the RFCC.
- Joshua Huffman earned the rank of Eagle Scout.

### JUNE

- C.J. Wax, Rockport Mayor, welcomed James Doughty-Munoz and Angela, his wife, to Rockport at the RFCC Visitor's Center. Doughty-Munoz's great-great-great grandfather, James Doughty, was one of Rockport's Founders.
- AC Commissioners honored Charlie Marshall with *Charlie Marshall Day* in AC.
- The Rockport City Council approved the Tule Creek West lease with Aransas Pathways.
- Joseph Patek, ACISD Superintendent, was named *Education Service Center, Region 2, Superintendent of the Year*.
- The Cedar Bayou dredging project received a $3 million boost from the State.
- MP wrote a column about his parents' 60th Wedding Anniversary.
- *Rockport Glory*, sculpted by Nic Noblique, was installed on TxDOT property south of McDonalds.
- The gazebo, a class project of Leadership Aransas County Class XVII, was completed for the History Center for AC.

# 30 YEARS THROUGH THE NEWS/LENS

Three generations of the Copano Causeway can be seen in this photo. From front to back, the original causeway, now used as a fishing pier; the current causeway; and the new causeway under construction.

## JULY

- Coldwell Banker–The Ron Brown Co. moved into its new home, the former RFCC building.
- The RFCC Membership Event garnered 175 new members. Richard Dias was the *Godfadda*, for the second time.
- Jarred Keith Wright was killed in a motorcycle accident at the intersection of Business SH 35 and Jim Smokehouse Road.
- First United Methodist Church sought the partial closure of St. Mary's Street to expand First Learning Tree, an early childhood learning center. *The council eventually approved the closure and First Learning Tree opened its expanded facilities in August 2014.*
- De McLallen was named *Citizen of the Year* at the RFCC's annual banquet.
- Coastal Care EMS opened.
- Chuck Steward, writer and photographer for RP, passed away suddenly.

## 2013: YEAR THIRTY

- Dorothy "Dot" LeBlanc, Boiling Pot's owner, passed away.
- Rex Hoyt, III signed a letter of intent to play baseball at Coastal Bend College.

### AUGUST
- Vandals hit 20 businesses along Business SH 35.
- The Humane Society and Adoption Center of Rockport-Fulton celebrated its 25th Anniversary.
- MP wrote a column about his youngest daughter getting married to Cody Lynch.
- Kimmy's Nail Salon opened.
- The Texas General Land Office awarded AC an additional $1 million for the dredging of Cedar Bayou and Vinson Slough.

### SEPTEMBER
- Skye Harvey, 20, was found dead in her home of an apparent gunshot wound. Her husband fled to Nacogdoches County with their five-month old son. He was charged with the murder and brought back to AC.
- Mike Donoho was hired as the City of Rockport's new Public Works Director, replacing Billy Dick, who retired after 23 years of service.
- The new Live Oak Learning Center officially opened its doors. A christening of the ship ceremony honoring Buster Gillis, former principal, included Pam Waters, Gillis' daughter-in-law, and Jenny Butler, his granddaughter.
- The writing team of Miles Arceneaux debuted their new novel, *LaSalle's Ghost*.
- The *Warriors Weekend Heroes Cup Fishing Tournament* for wounded servicemen was held in Rockport-Fulton.
- Aransas Pathways held a groundbreaking ceremony for the Castro Nature Sanctuary.

# 30 YEARS THROUGH THE NEWS/LENS

The RFHS Bonfire returned to Rockport Beach in 2013.

- The new Fulton Learning Center was officially dedicated.
- The RFHS Bonfire returned to Rockport Beach.

**OCTOBER**

- The Texas Historical Foundation Grants Committee gave $5,000 to fund the book, *Aransas County in Postcards*, to be sold as a fundraiser for the History Center for Aransas County.
- The Rockport City Trailways was formed as a new local Volkssport Club in association with the Texas Volkssport Association.
- Martin Chadwick, 54, and Denis Barsness, 72, died of injuries they received during an assault in their home on Enterprise Boulevard.
- A historical marker was unveiled for the Wood-Jackson House.

## 2013: YEAR THIRTY

- AC Motorsports opened.
- The Cedar Bayou/Vinson Slough Dredging Project went out for bids.
- *Birds in Art*, world-renowned exhibit, was on display at the RCA.
- RCC residents voiced opposition to a proposed upscale RV park abutting the south side of the subdivision.
- Local, state, and federal agencies worked together in the arrest of three people associated with Q Spa in Harbor Oaks Village Shopping Center, who were involved in an international human trafficking ring and the promotion of prostitution.

## NOVEMBER

- Sacred Heart Catholic Church dedicated its renovated church.
- TxDOT approved spending $200,000 for the development of an AC Airport Master Plan.
- Jimmy Kendrick, Fulton Mayor, gave the *"Googles" Cole Legacy Award* to Dorothy "Dot" LeBlanc, late owner of the Boiling Pot, posthumously, for her support and work in Fulton.
- HEB celebrated its 50th Anniversary in Rockport and donated $22,500 to various organizations.
- E.E. "Dunny" Dunsworth, a longtime community volunteer, passed away.
- Ground was broken for the new Cantwell's Auto Sales on the SH 35 Bypass.
- The RFHS varsity volleyball team made history by winning the UIL Regional Quarterfinals.
- AC Commissioners announced plans to build a new road in

# 30 YEARS THROUGH THE NEWS/LENS

Lamar connecting Bois D'Arc to Seaside Loop, which gave the Lamar VFD easier access to SH 35.

- Rockport Wellness Center opened.

**DECEMBER**

- Wade Sinard, RFHS tennis coach, was selected *Corpus Christi Tennis Association's Coach of the Year* for the second consecutive year.
- William Adams, AC Court-At-Law Judge, announced he would seek reelection in the 2014 GOP Primary. *Richard Bianchi, AC Attorney, defeated Adams.*
- The TPWD announced plans to replace the fence around the Big Tree in Lamar.
- Sandy Jumper, RFCC Director of Tourism, received the *Texas Coastal Bend Tourism Council's Tourism Award*.
- The Rotary Club of Rockport distributed Webster's Dictionaries to every third grader at Live Oak Learning Center.

# Acknowledgements

*To my wife Diane,*
    my best friend and partner in everything I've done the past 30-plus years. You've supported me and have always been by my side during good times and in bad. You're the Christian woman I always hoped I would meet. You helped keep me on the path whenever I started to veer. There's no doubt in my mind God knew what he was doing when he brought us together at the food court in Post Oak Mall. Our life together is full of wonderful memories, and I look forward to the rest of our lives together, however it plays out. I don't know what the future holds, but I know God will always carry us in his loving hands. I love you with all of my heart Peanut.

*To Alyssa and Ashlee,*
    my two precious daughters. Ya'll have brought nothing but joy...okay, I can't lie, there were some periods of stress! Y'all have been a huge part of my life since the day God granted me the privilege of being called "Dad." Now that both of you are part of a growing family, you can begin to understand how much joy each of you brought into my life. I may no longer be "your man," but I'll always be your dad.

# 30 YEARS THROUGH THE NEWS/LENS

*To my sons-in-law Doug and Cody,*
> I couldn't be happier with the choices Alyssa and Ashlee made. As good Christian men, I know y'all will always take care of my girls. I know you will be great fathers. Keep Christ in your homes, lead your family, and lean on your faith. One final request…could y'all let me win at golf at least once?

*To my parents,*
> without whom I wouldn't be around to write this book. I challenged y'all a lot during my formative years, but you always gave the proper guidance. The Christian home you provided helped mold me, and had a huge influence on the man I am now. Thank you for the sacrifices you made for our family. While I was busy trying to provide Alyssa and Ashlee with some of the material things I didn't have growing up, I tried to make sure I gave them all the things I did have—those things, which really count. Your unconditional love was always felt.

*To my brother and two sisters,*
> I couldn't have asked for better siblings. Each of your personalities is forever forged in a part of me. I would not be who I am today—whether you want to take credit, or blame—without each of y'all in my life.

*To my mother-in-law and late father-in-law,*
> thanks for accepting a skinny German boy into your Italian family. I know I was a little shock to your system, but you always showed your love and support in your special way.

*To all my employees through the years,*
> especially the late Florence Sharp who stood by my side

## ACKNOWLEDGEMNENTS

during my early years at the *Rockport Pilot* when I was learning the ropes, and ruffling a lot of feathers in the office with the changes I implemented. To my current employees, I can't thank you enough. Publishing a community newspaper is a labor of love, and each of you, my long-tenured sidekicks, have made coming to work a joy—whatever the hour! I don't know any boss who has a better work "family."

*To Dup,*
my good friend and surrogate Rockport dad. You will never know how much our countless "talks" through the years helped guide me. You should consider writing a book called "Dup-isms."

*To everyone who has helped me along the way in my newspaper career,* including the late Don Chandler, whose guidance pointed me in the right direction during my first three years in Brenham; Charles Moser, longtime editor and publisher of the *Brenham Banner-Press*, and my first boss; Clyde King, Hartman Newspaper's president, friend, and half-decent Elvis impersonator; and last, but certainly not least, the men in the Hartman family—Bill, Fred, and Lee. There aren't many folks who can say they worked for the same company/family their entire career. Thank you all for your support and guidance the past three decades.

*To the late Fred Hartman,*
I would not be in the newspaper business today had it not been for a chance he took in 1984, giving me the opportunity to run one of his newspapers at the age of 24. I learned a lot from "The Leader" during the first third of my career. One of the best bits of advice he gave came at a time when I was feeling down about

what some people were saying about me. He said, "Son, as long as you're in this business there are always going to be people who hate you. Your goal is that when they look into your casket they say, 'I hated that @#$@@$*, but he was fair.'"

**SPECIAL THANKS**

# *Special Thanks...*

*This was my first attempt
at writing/publishing a book,
and let's just say, it's a little bit different
than putting together
a newspaper twice per week!*

*Dawn Gwin of Dawn Gwin Studio* guided me through the process, and put in many hours as each deadline neared. This book wouldn't have been printed in time for the initial book signing without her expertise. What could have been a disastrous experience, turned into a great one, based in large part to her skill in her field.

*Vickie Moon Merchant, a member of Friends of the History Center for Aransas County,* put in countless hours editing some of the "rawer" copy for this book, and put in countless hours developing the Newseum of Aransas County exhibit. It was a special experience to work closely with her because I lived in her mother's home for the first few weeks I lived in Rockport. Johnnie, her mother, was a real blessing for me, especially during my first year in Rockport.

*To Jackie Shaw, Pam Stranahan, and Carla Rinche, members of the book/exhibit committee,* thanks for all your work and support.

It's done!

Made in the USA
San Bernardino, CA
08 October 2014